CODESTINY

ATLEE VALENTINE POPE
AND GEORGE F. BROWN, JR.

CODESTINY

Overcome Your Growth Challenges by
Helping Your Customers Overcome Theirs

GREENLEAF
BOOK GROUP PRESS

Published by Greenleaf Book Group Press
Austin, Texas
www.gbgpress.com

Distributed by Greenleaf Book Group LLC

For ordering information or special discounts for bulk purchases, please contact Greenleaf Book Group LLC at PO Box 91869, Austin, TX 78709, 512.891.6100.

Design and composition by Greenleaf Book Group LLC and Alex Head
Cover design by Greenleaf Book Group LLC

Publisher's Cataloging-In-Publication Data
(Prepared by The Donohue Group, Inc.)

Pope, Atlee Valentine.
    CoDestiny : overcome your growth challenges by helping your customers overcome theirs / Atlee Valentine Pope and George F. Brown, Jr. -- 1st ed.

    p. ; cm.

    ISBN: 978-1-60832-053-0

    1. Business logistics. 2. Corporations--Growth. 3. Relationship marketing. I. Brown, George F., Jr. II. Title.

HD38.5.P66 2010
658.5   2010929171

Part of the Tree Neutral™ program, which offsets the number of trees consumed in the production and printing of this book by taking proactive steps, such as planting trees in direct proportion to the number of trees used: www.treeneutral.com

Printed in the United States of America on acid-free paper

10 11 12 13 14 15   10 9 8 7 6 5 4 3 2 1

First Edition

CONTENTS

FOREWORD

While mired in the depths of the 2001-2002 global recession, Emerson devoted time to rethinking a number of key customer relationships that confounded our managers. We observed the waning willingness of customers to acknowledge and reward our distinctiveness contrasted with their heavy appetite for our capacities—the technology, support, and continuity of supply offered by our company over decades. This threatened our prospects for future sales and profits and demanded a response. Growth continued to pose our greatest challenge.

In searching for an answer, we uncovered little theory and less practical insight as to how and why such large and important partners so adroitly minimized our role. Fortunately, we found the leaders of Blue Canyon Partners, Atlee Valentine Pope and George F. Brown, Jr., who shared our fascination with this problem and offered their help. Through years of research, conceptual development, and practical application, an approach to resolving these conditions emerged. *CoDestiny* shares this development with you, and more important, the tools and processes underlying George and Atlee's approach.

Logic underpins their thoughts. The information revolution of the late twentieth century and the creation of sourcing tools allowed procurement professionals to aggressively drive down prices by suppressing differentiation among suppliers in the bidding process. Globalization expanded the base of potential suppliers, bringing forth new competitors with radically different cost bases and agendas. Traditional supplier relationships unraveled, wringing profitability from the supply base, and with it, suppliers' means for future investment in capabilities. However, this evolution ignores two nearly universal facts. In industry after industry, unsolved needs continue to saddle end-users, regardless of the users' willingness to sensibly pay for advancements that satisfy these demands. Furthermore, the torturous path of supplying a product or service—from raw materials through assembly, to distribution and installation, all the way to the end-user applying the product over its life—harbors inefficiencies to attack.

Typically, the major industry players control this dialogue within an industry and enjoy varied success in driving progress. Many savor this control and lack incentive to alter the landscape. This creates a precarious situation for these leaders and, unfortunately, for those suppliers that attach their fate to them. As new technologies and global opponents catalyze shifts in the competitive balance, this evolution threatens the hesitant.

Opposing these threats and exploiting opportunities requires a deep understanding of the entire industry system as well as the ability to craft a basis of cooperation across key players. Each constituent must shoulder a role, contribute, and, most of all, realize the fruits of the labor. Competing in today's world of technology and change requires selfless determination and strong collaboration across multiple organizations, a fact that often conflicts with business cultures and expectations.

This reality implores managers to systematically investigate their roles in a given industry in the context of their key relationships, and to act upon their conclusions. In *CoDestiny*, George and Atlee provide a template for this entire process. From mapping an industry to searching for value levers, their experience will enlighten and illustrate the foundations of their assessments. More important, the book's thoughts on relationships will aid in the execution of the plans and the realization of effective partnerships essential to success.

As you read *CoDestiny*, you will learn a structured approach to this multifaceted problem. In applying the book's process, the number of opportunities it exposes will surprise you. Finally, you will confront choices. Which of your customers and suppliers linked in this journey comprehends the potential and/or will readily share the risks and rewards? Some relationships will perish, but for learned reasons. With the chosen ones, however, you will share a vision and a path laden with potential—a common destiny.

—Charles A. Peters

Senior Executive Vice President

and Member of the Board of Directors, Emerson

INTRODUCTION

Sustainable, profitable growth is a constant priority for any business. But the initiatives that drove yesterday's successes often cannot deliver results today or tomorrow. As companies arrive at this crossroads, where expectations are high but their economic future is unclear, leaders must hunt for tactics, approaches, and methods that will help them navigate toward sustainable prosperity.

Suppliers who sell to other businesses are particularly challenged. These business-to-business firms often face complex markets with varying needs, demands, and economic drivers. Dilemmas over such issues as commoditization, industry consolidation, price-based competition, and complicated channel networks can thwart growth and inhibit success. At the same time, opportunities to enter new areas of business, acquire companies, and nurture major customer relationships can reenergize the organization's growth. Simply put, for these companies, sustaining and growing the business is a big-time opportunity—and also a big-time challenge.

Over the last two decades, we've had the privilege of working with many industry-leading business-to-business organizations on their strategies in the toughest, most competitive markets around the world. These firms have invited us to help them solve their most pressing, perplexing problems. What their leaders needed was an entirely new approach—one that would let their organizations thrive in the face of ever-changing market realities. Our response has been to help refocus their perspective, by offering a method that allows businesses to successfully create value for customers and capture value for themselves. In other words, a firm can overcome its growth challenges by helping its customers overcome theirs. Ultimately, the firm can succeed by linking its destiny with that of its customers.

Before we can discover ideas that will bring value to a firm and help it grow, we must bring these ideas to the customers who will reward the firm for this value. But these rewards can be fleeting and elusive, particularly as the definition of a "valuable" product or service varies from customer to customer. And yet opportunities to overcome these growth challenges by creating new value opportunities don't just happen haphazardly at the mercy of market forces. Rather, there is an approach by which this can be achieved systematically and consistently.

In this book, we'll describe a systematic approach to overcoming your growth challenges by creating value for customers and capturing value for your business. Our approach works for any business, from start-up to market leader. It works with any product line, in any industry, in any location. We've presented this approach in three sections, each building on the foundations of the last.

In the first section of the book, we'll show you how to create and capture value. You'll discover how to define your customer chains and segment your customers according to the motives that drive their purchase decisions—and you'll understand why you must do both for the success of your business. You'll learn how to convert your ideas into actions for which your customer will reward you.

In the second section, we'll show you how to develop a specific growth strategy for going to market—a strategy that accelerates your growth and captures value for your business by focusing on products, service, price, acquisitions, market expansion, and external relationships.

In the third section, we'll show you how to implement your Go-to-Market Strategy with a Get-to-Market Plan, so you can take action and increase your shareholder value as quickly as possible.

Throughout the book, we mix theoretical discussions with practical case studies. In our fifty combined years of advising companies, we've found that we learn the most valuable lessons from our experiences with a variety of strong companies in diverse industries and countries. We believe that these lessons from other environments can be as valuable to our readers as they have been to us. It is our hope that you will take these ideas and use them to succeed with your business.

—Atlee Valentine Pope and George F. Brown, Jr.

SECTION I: CREATE AND CAPTURE VALUE THROUGH YOUR CUSTOMER CHAIN

Chapter 1

YOUR CUSTOMERS WANT MORE—
AND THEY WILL PAY FOR IT

When we are called in to speak confidentially with companies about their growth challenges, business leaders rarely share with us that they have a crystal clear, perfect understanding of their marketplace. Instead, they often lament that their customers and markets seem unnecessarily mystifying, brazenly unforgiving, and overly harsh. We hear complaints such as "Our products are not a commodity, but our customers treat us as if they were," or "Our channel partners are blood-sucking weasels who do little to promote our efforts," or even "Our most cherished customers are now dictating that we enter into reverse auction bids to ensure price competition." Without a doubt, these growth-inhibiting pressures are real and unrelenting, and they should not be ignored.

Several years ago, we had the opportunity to work with Emerson, the diversified manufacturing firm widely recognized today for its excellence in engineering and management. A number of Emerson's companies make products like motors, valves, compressors, and control systems that are sold into the appliance, furnace and air conditioner, and water heater industries.

During our first meeting with Emerson leadership, we heard stressful comments. "They treat us like a commodity," said one company leader who observed how customers, in decision after decision, rejected Emerson's newer innovations in favor of lower-cost standard products. Another executive noted, "If an idea costs a dime more, it gets rejected unless we're willing to fund it out of our own pocket." At the time, Emerson enjoyed a leading market position in these industries, yet given these customer behaviors, some individuals had doubts about Emerson's long-term viability. The question posed at the end of the meeting summarized the group's concern: "How can we, on the one hand, enjoy a number-one market share position with these customers and, on the other hand, be treated with such indifference?"

To help Emerson unravel this complex paradox, we interviewed a variety of players in the appliance, furnace and air conditioner, and water heater markets. We spoke with employees of Emerson companies and to their customers, including distributors, retailers, contractors, home builders, and even end customers using these products. These individuals spanned multiple job functions, from general management to operations to purchasing to marketing to sales. Our goal: to learn from various customers how Emerson could potentially bring value to the table—value that depended less on a product's price than on its benefits, and that would be eagerly recognized and handsomely rewarded.

Based on these interviews, we reported to Emerson a message that has often emerged from our decades of field research: *Your customers want more—and they will pay for it!* This finding differs radically from the perception of being treated "like a commodity" and from the belief that an idea would be "rejected if it costs a dime more." But in fact, the conclusion is accurate.

We've learned that *customers want more and will pay for it* in market after market, from one product line to another. And to readers who reflect on their own personal experiences, this conclusion shouldn't come as a surprise. Who among us hasn't jumped at the opportunity to buy, say, a higher-priced car—once the carmakers began to include sunroofs, advanced safety features, and such great consumer electronics as DVD players and GPS mapping? Others of us rushed to buy wide-screen, flat-panel TVs at prices an order of magnitude higher than what we'd spent for the TV being replaced. Still others of us were among the consumers fascinated with granite countertops, outdoor kitchens, and monstrous master bathrooms. And few of us can deny that we've willingly paid more than $3 for the "Starbucks experience" when there were much lower-priced cups of coffee just around the corner.

All these examples show that customers recognize value and are willing to pay for that value. Successful firms tap into those customers' needs. They follow a systematic approach to *creating value* for their customers and *capturing value* for themselves in order to grow—and to reach greater heights of success, your organization must do the same. You must align your business's destiny with that of your customers. To do this, you must accept that your business's interests are intertwined with that of your customers' and that both have a common destiny. You must learn how to identify your customers and how to determine what they value. You must discover how to create value, not only for consumers but for suppliers, channel partners, and other organizations with which you have key relationships. You must develop a Go-to-Market Strategy and a Get-to-Market Plan that will help you capture value. And, most important, you must learn how to implement your plan immediately and reward your stockholders as quickly as possible.

We know only too well that discussing theory without taking action is a waste of time.

So let's take action.

In our work with Emerson, we embarked on an interesting investigative journey that would lead us to uncover an amazing variety of market messages. An executive from a major appliance company started us off by explaining one of the ongoing challenges associated with energy and water use: "Consumers are more and more aware of energy and water and are looking for more efficiency in all their appliance purchases. We have to offer steady progress on these fronts. We invest heavily in technologies that use less energy and water."

Energy and water were what he called the "table stakes" of the industry. To maintain its position as a "major player" and the "first-to-mind leader," the appliance manufacturer had to meet customers' expectations by continually delivering improvements in energy and water use and developing smarter, time-saving appliances. According to this executive, breakthroughs in these areas could be game changers—innovations that would motivate consumers to replace their existing washers and dryers long before these appliances simply quit working. He observed, "If the clothes came out of the dryer already folded, we wouldn't even have to advertise."

A very different story about replacing appliances emerged in discussions with the manager of a big-box home center. We met with him at one of the company's flagship stores, and as we discussed water heaters, he walked us behind the store to show us the "graveyard." There we saw about a dozen water heaters stacked for pickup by a waste removal company. Most of them looked brand-new. The manager explained that the units had been purchased over the past few weeks, some by contractors and some by do-it-yourselfers, and returned shortly there-after. "Pretty much all of them were fine when they left the store," he grumbled, "but they got trashed during installation." The store's policy was to accept returns basically without argument, and it would cost more to repair these units than they were worth, so they just went to the graveyard for disposal.

Later, in conversations with contractors, we asked about this prob-lem. One contractor's company had more than a dozen trucks out, all doing various types of appliance installations, day in and day out. He told us that stuff happens during installation:

> Sometimes it's just a dumb mistake. Sometimes it's a wrong hookup. Sometimes it's a problem in the house that goes unnoticed. And with installers working on a tight schedule and trying to finish all the jobs that we've committed to for the day, we know there are going to be problems now and then. The worst thing about it? It creates callbacks, and callbacks kill us. We don't get paid for a second visit to fix a problem, and sometimes it requires a third visit because we have to go and get a new unit. And some of these calls come at night or on the weekend, when we pay double for overtime, which adds even more expense to the job. Any job that involves a callback is a profit killer.

A sales executive at a furnace and air-conditioning system manu-facturer talked instead about price pressures. While he acknowledged the major appliance executive's theory—that an innovation could get a consumer to spend more money by trading up—he noted that a significant part of his sales were to home builders. "These customers are brutal," he confided. "They buy in quantity, but they want rock-bottom prices, and rarely will they go beyond the basic products." The sales exec went on to say, "About the only time we can bring new technology out, and see some uplift in prices, is when the government mandates higher standards for the industry."

To deepen our understanding, we talked with a number of home builders. They pointed out that they make the HVAC decisions long before the ultimate customer shows up, and they insisted that home buyers don't really care which system is in the house. One home builder challenged us—and the major appliance executive's claim—by asking, "Do you know what brand of furnace is in your house?"

In addition to this argument, we heard a wide spectrum of messages about costs—of the components inside the appliance and of the appliances themselves. One water heater manufacturer joked, "Most people think all we do is bend metal and shoot screws. They think all the value and all the costs are in the components, like the motors and control systems inside these appliances that we buy from suppliers." At the other end of the spectrum were the firms that handled the installation of furnace and air-conditioning systems. From these firms' perspective, even the costs of the full HVAC system, let alone any component within it, were modest in comparison to the costs of the labor and service involved in the installation process.

Along with these messages from appliance manufacturers, sellers, and installers and from home builders, we also heard from homeowners. We learned that while these consumers expected to see fair prices, they spent far more time discussing their concerns about what features they *weren't* getting. One cluster of consumers had strong opinions about safety, and another group focused on the reliability of these products. They shared their desire for assurance that their water heater wasn't going to leak and destroy their property, and they revealed their worries about what would happen when storms and other power disruptions triggered an unwanted electrical surge in the appliance.

One focus group participant whose family had just replaced its furnace and air conditioner described how much the new system was saving them in electricity costs. Others in the group jumped right into this discussion, revealing that they too were interested in efficiency and comfort features. Someone spoke up about how great it would be to be able to turn things off and on through the Internet when he was away from his home. The innovation theory was on the table once again.

When we returned to meet with the Emerson executives, it was with the following conclusion: Some of the firm's customers did in fact consider certain Emerson products to be a commodity, and regardless of the promise of improved features, those customers still wouldn't pay a dime more. But other customers were excited about the great ideas on the drawing boards at Emerson's many research and development centers and would jump enthusiastically at the opportunity to buy such products.

From this research, we determined that Emerson's customers associated value with such concepts as water and energy savings (for the homeowner), increased convenience and reliability (for the homeowner), elimination of callbacks (for the contractor), decreased warranty returns (for the store manager), and increased opportunities for trading up (for the sales exec). Different customers made it very clear that they wouldn't hesitate to purchase an offering that delivered value along such lines. In other words, our message to Emerson was "Your customers *want* more—and they will pay for it."

Of course, our conclusion brings with it a number of challenges. The first of these is to define what creates value—and to identify which customers will pay you for this value. Over the years, we've become conscious of the many great ideas that emerge from company laboratories, sales team meetings, and other sources, only to meet the market's reaction of complete disinterest and disregard. Every business leader can give examples of ideas that were good for some customer segments but totally inappropriate for others.

The subsequent question, which occurs even when it becomes clear what product or service creates value for which customer, is how to define a well-honed, carefully crafted response to this challenge—in other words, how to help both you and your customers grow by creating value for them and capturing value for your firm.

Sometimes firms can quickly deliver value once they know of their customers' needs and interests. In other instances, however, creating value is not so simple. An appropriate response to the customer's needs may require significant investment in product development, a lengthy lead time to introduce the next-generation product, or other demands for advanced technology.

Emerson was able to embed sensors and re-engineer controls to respond to the homeowners' concerns about safety, efficiency, and the reliability of water heaters. The company also deepened its involvement with contractors by enhancing both direct support and creating retrofit diagnostic packages that predict failure and ease system repairs. As Emerson implemented these concepts, it was able to deliver value to its own customers and be rewarded. Because these upgrades responded to customer preferences, they yielded gains in volume and earnings. Additionally, because new, higher-priced technologies such as the "idiot-proof" installation components were embraced by contractors, over time they were put into the product specifications.

Over the years, we've witnessed many creative, successful responses from companies that help them gain insight into value creation. From introducing customer-centric technical innovations to becoming the partner of choice within a new channel network to establishing a global footprint across developing regions, companies have met their customers' unmet needs and have delivered value, allowing them to grow and prosper.

In this book, we'll share how a packaging firm captured value through a groundbreaking design that, by providing unique displays for retailers, helped the customer gain shelf space. We'll showcase a business-to-business supplier's successful entry into the Chinese market after tapping into a network of preferred channel partners that needed technical support to penetrate more remote, lesser developed Chinese cities. We'll describe how a supplier of commercial vehicle components, by forging relationships with logistics fleets, helped its truck builder customers gain market share. And in other examples, we'll illustrate how companies have managed to avoid zero-sum price negotiations and instead win higher volume with a superior product—priced so that both they and their customers can gain market share.

Once you've read the book, you and your company can overcome your growth challenges by creating win-win-win opportunities across the marketplace. You will be on the road to achieving your co-destiny: shared success.

Chapter 2

DEFINE YOUR CUSTOMER CHAIN

Business leaders must always worry about prices and margins. "How can we sustain margins in the face of price pressures from both purchasing groups and competitors?" is a question we get frequently from clients. Ensuring that your customers remain profitable customers is always a challenge, and especially so in today's highly competitive world. The starting point for understanding how to create and capture value is the customer chain.

"How can we grow?" is a question we hear even more often. Today's firms have designed processes to identify and prioritize growth opportunities. Businesses around the globe have created entire paradigms to help them think through growth options in a logical, structured manner. In the past several years, we've seen a proliferation of innovation centers and other business units whose mission is to get beyond the day-to-day challenges and position their firms for the future. These types of efforts have paid considerable dividends, but CEOs nonetheless continue to rank top-line growth among their most critical challenges.[1]

---

1. The Conference Board, *CEO Challenge 2007: Top 10 Challenges* (October 2007). Top-line growth was ranked the top challenge in 2006. In 2007, it was ranked second; according to CEOs from North America it was the greatest challenge that year, and according to CEOs from both Europe and Asia it was the second-greatest.

Fundamentally, we're convinced that companies are best positioned to understand their growth opportunities by understanding their customer chains. The customer chain structures provide crucial information about the pathways, partners, and customers that must be brought into the growth process.

We also frequently hear the question "How do we keep ahead of the competition?" Facing innovative and aggressive challenges from both traditional and unexpected competitors is a constant reality for successful firms. One executive who is responsible for her firm's new business development described her job as "distracting the competition from our current customers." While firms exhort the virtues of top-line growth, business leaders also recognize that there is much to lose if a competitor succeeds in converting a current customer. Over and over, our studies find that unexpected competition results from a new or evolving customer chain within the market, and that aggressive efforts to stay ahead of this evolution are crucial to competitive success.

In response to threats from competition, the customer chain consistently provides the foundation for eventual success. For example, most firms know the "usual suspect" competitors quite well, encountering them in the market essentially every day. This familiarity allows businesses to thwart certain predictable advances. It is the unexpected competitor, however, that causes disruption by catching a firm unprepared. Studying the Customer Chain Map can provide insights about these potential new competitors, especially when a new pathway emerges on the map or when market-entry strategies involve new connections along the customer chain.

We observed one such situation when a specialist distributor recognized that it was in a position of strength. Its end customer relationships were strong, and its logistics structures were capable of supporting an expanded product line. The distributor developed new supply sources, broadened its catalog, and became a major source of competition for the generalist distributors that had previously served these end markets. The company's strategy—incorporating new supply sources into its existing customer chain structure, so it could take new products to existing markets and customers—allowed it to grow. Its competitors might have anticipated this initiative had they, too, recognized the missing link on the customer chain.

Most customer chains are complex. Our interviews with participants in the appliances and HVAC market (described in the previous chapter) outlined a number of customer chains. The discussion of water heaters, for example, reflected a customer chain that was five stages long, from the component supplier to the water heater manufacturer to the dealer to the installer and finally to the consumer.

Figure 2.1: Five-Stage Customer Chain Map

The customer chain picture in figure 2.1 is typical of those seen in business markets, where it is also typical for firms to be involved in numerous and distinct structures of this type. Another example from the previous chapter would be home builders managing new construction projects and homeowners making decisions about appliance replacements—two separate customer chains, both served by furnace and air-conditioning companies.

By studying the customer chains that exist in business markets, a firm can garner insights on both existing and new pathways to market. This is especially true in environments where change is under way because of industry consolidation, global expansion, technology migration, or any number of other drivers of change. Customer chains provide a framework, and the company determines how to connect its products and services to other participants within that structure, from its direct customer to intermediaries to the consumer of the end product.

CUSTOMER CHAIN FEATURES: MULTIPLICITY AND INTERDEPENDENCE

Two critical features of customer chains can help a business develop plans to overcome its growth challenge by capturing the value it creates for its customer. The first is *multiplicity*—in most business markets, there are multiple customers along the customer chain. Each looks back along the chain to make decisions about suppliers and also looks forward along the chain to define its marketing and sales strategy. The multiplicity of customers along the full length of the customer chain offers distinct opportunities to create value. In the next chapter, we'll provide some fascinating success stories that have emerged during efforts to learn from the more distant stages of the customer chain.

The second feature is *interdependence*—the realization that a customer chain can only be as strong as its weakest link. We encourage our clients to think about not just win–win partnerships but also win–win–win relationships—those with more than two successful outcomes. Any participant in a customer chain who fails to see the value in participating is unlikely to participate—or at best, will do so without enthusiasm or effort. But our focus on creating value to capture value in order for all parties to grow provides a mechanism for sharing the win all along the customer chain, as a means of motivating enthusiastic collaboration.

CUSTOMER CHAIN DESCRIPTIONS

There are many types of business-to-business customer chains. Some firms—for example, parts and components manufacturers, packaging manufacturers, and chemical and feedstock suppliers—sell to other manufacturers (their direct customers), who subsequently use these purchases in their own manufacturing process and then sell their own product to the next link on the customer chain. This is the case for companies like Emerson, which provides motors, control systems, and the like to manufacturers of appliances, water heaters, and other products.

Other suppliers—such as medical equipment manufacturers, office equipment manufacturers, and tool and equipment companies—sell their products to sales channel partners (their direct customers), who in turn sell, deliver, install, or integrate these products and services for customers further along the customer chain, often in conjunction with other products and services. Examples in the previous chapter of these types of intermediaries range from big-box retailers to HVAC installers and service companies. It is not unusual for a firm to belong to a customer chain that includes many intermediaries, each with a distinct role and its own business model.

A typical marketplace cultivates many different customer chains, some extending for many stages. Most markets involve not just multiple but distinct pathways. One of our clients, a global automotive parts manufacturer, could identify more than seven hundred separate customer chain pathways to the market. Another, an agricultural food industry supplier, faced seven stages along the customer chain before its product eventually reached the end customer.

In business-to-business markets, some of the relationships along the customer chain are quite significant; we worked with one supplier-customer relationship that spanned six product lines, covered four continents, and involved annual sales of nearly $1 billion. Some relationships involve a sequential manufacturing process, while others involve channels through which a manufacturer's products go to market. Within a single organization, also, there can be several stages of the customer chain, reflecting the various business functions that are involved in key decision-making processes—purchasing, engineering, manufacturing, sales, and so on. We mapped out the customer chains of one client, a component supplier to the automotive industry, and found that its relationship structures differed radically from one carmaker to the next. This had major implications for the firm's ability to identify opportunities for value creation.

In our approach—overcoming growth challenges by creating value for customers and then capturing it for shareholders—we believe that carefully mapping the customer chains that exist within a market is the first step. It is critical to look at every stage of the customer chain. It is critical to analyze every pathway that exists (and that might emerge) linking the participants from one end of the chain to the other. Typically, there are alternate pathways in a market; they differ from one competitor to the next, and even from one segment to the next (whether by geography, by vertical market, or by some other characteristic). Not only that, but the pathways change over time, often rapidly.

In our strategy work, the customer chain is a remarkable and consistent source of "ah-ha" moments. Sometimes, especially when markets are evolving and changing, just the careful depiction of the Customer Chain Map yields important insights. This was the case with a medical equipment firm that saw in the customer chain structure the distinction between its path to market and that of its main competitor. The firm was quickly able to understand that its model was poorly aligned with the needs of certain customers further along the chain. Constructing the Customer Chain Map helped one packaging supplier realize that its channels didn't connect to certain end customers. An electrical equipment provider made a crucial discovery: Though it had been targeting certain participants as growth markets along its preferred pathway, those participants didn't even exist in several countries.

USING CUSTOMER CHAINS TO FIND GROWTH OPPORTUNITIES: THE WEAKEST LINK

The customer chain can identify opportunities for value creation (and ultimately, growth) in two major ways. The first involves the "weakest link" concept. The customer chain involves a sequence of businesses (or, in the case of stages within a single firm, decision makers). At each stage of the customer chain, the business is going to make a decision by asking, "Which supplier and which purchase option is the best for me?" For the supplier, as we've described earlier, achieving success basically requires that its offer create a win at each stage of the customer chain.

When there is a "weak link"—a stage where the competitor's offer is preferred or where participation is not seen as a business priority—the odds are slim that the supplier will realize success. By spotting weak links, therefore, a supplier can usually identify unserved or underserved markets. These are the segments with the potential to become growth markets—if the supplier can create the necessary value.

The packaging supplier mentioned above served the food industry; it created a strong presence in restaurants and grocery stores by selling food storage and packaging products through foodservice distributors across the United States. Its most significant customer chain is depicted in figure 2.2.

Figure 2.2: Packaging Customer Chain Map

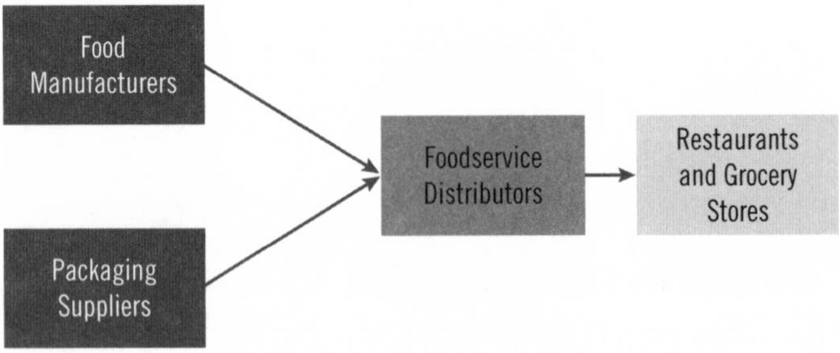

Over time, however, shifts took place in the structure of the pack-ager's market. Food manufacturers began to prepackage ready-to-serve food items, which they sold to the same restaurants and grocery stores through the same foodservice distributors. Basically, these manufac-turers reclaimed the preparation and packaging function from the restaurant or grocery store. No longer did the grocery store prepare the ready-to-serve food items using plastic containers, wrap, and other materials purchased from the packaging supplier. Instead, this food was prepared, wrapped, and sealed by the food manufacturer and then shipped to the grocer to be put directly on the shelf. As we worked with the packaging firm, it learned that competing suppliers were participating in a new, nontraditional customer chain, depicted below:

Figure 2.3: Nontraditional Packaging Customer Chain Map

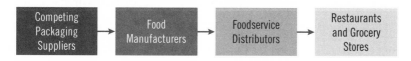

By mapping the changing customer chains within this market, we were able to identify our client's weak link—namely, the lack of a channel to the food manufacturers. Once this weak link was recognized, the packaging firm was able to start the process of determining how to create greater value for the food manufacturing segment, which up to this point it had failed to serve.

USING CUSTOMER CHAINS TO FIND GROWTH OPPORTUNITIES: KNOW THE PLAYERS

The second way in which the customer chain can identify opportunities for value creation is by helping an organization get acquainted with the other players up and down and across the customer chain. This requires a careful study of not only the stages directly adjacent to a supplier but also the stages at a greater distance. Our experience suggests that most firms have a solid understanding of their direct customers. After all, these are the customers they interact with, often many times a day. By the same token, many firms have insight on the final customers—those at the end of the customer chain—particularly to the extent that their product survives in some recognizable fashion even as it passes along the stages of the customer chain. A plumbing faucets and fixtures manufacturer, for example, may have close relationships with its distributors as well as clear insights about homeowners' perspectives. The same quality of insight and understanding is often lacking, however, when it comes to the other participants along this manufacturer's customer chain, such as the general contractors, the plumbing contractors and installers, and the home-building companies.

Understanding these customer chain participants can be important in many ways, not just in terms of spotlighting weak links or ferreting out new market segments. In working with a major manufacturer of high-technology equipment, we identified a customer chain structure within the marketplace that looked like figure 2.4.

Figure 2.4: High-Technology Equipment Customer Chain Map

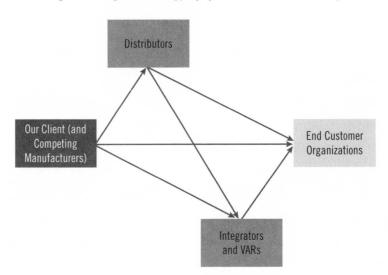

Basically, this firm and its competitors had distinct pathways into the market, involving both direct sales and sales through two distinct groups of intermediaries (distributors and integrators).[2] Not all the competitors used all the possible variants of these models. Our client, for example, did not have many integrator relationships. More important, the different categories of services varied widely across the vertical end-customer markets in terms of priority.

Our client's key realization was that its pathways to the market failed to provide critical services that were highly valued in certain end market segments. In some markets, particularly those in which end customers had a strong in-house technical staff, our client's products were highly regarded and typically the first choice. Yet the firm lost business when other potential end customers, for one reason or another, developed a reliance on a third-party integrator. As a result, it had essentially no presence in those end markets. Understanding each player along the customer chain—who it is, what it does, how it creates value, what drives its purchase decisions, what drives its own sales successes with customers further along the chain—can provide great insight on how a firm can create value for its customers and thus improve its own prospects for growth and profitability.

These simple examples highlight the understanding that a Customer Chain Map can contribute. Most customer chains are in fact far more complex. Consider the case of the specialty vehicle parts aftermarket, the segment of the parts market that provides everything from the auto parts featured in movies (think *The Fast and the Furious*) to truck accessories. Even the complex Customer Chain Map shown

---

2. Atlee Valentine Pope and George F. Brown, Jr., "Sales Models in Business Markets with Complex Customer Chains," *SBusiness* (Winter 2008).

in figure 2.5, in all its details, is oversimplified; in reality, a distinct map with distinct channels and end customers exists for virtually every one of this manufacturer's product categories, from truck towing accessories to mobile electronics.

Creating this Customer Chain Map led to a fountain of insights for this vehicle parts firm. Its leaders were able to identify new ways to grow the business with existing products in existing markets, simply by establishing critical new channel relationships. They were able to locate new end markets they were failing to reach because their channels did not currently connect. They were able to determine which products complemented existing channel relationships as well as their brand position among end customers. In all these ways, the Customer Chain Map provided the basis for organizing and analyzing a complex, multifaceted market.

A thorough analysis of the customer chain addresses the three major concerns of any business leader: margin management, revenue enhancement, and competitive positioning. While the specific challenges differ for each company, the solutions always require insights into the customer chains that present opportunities for growth through establishing a co-destiny—one that achieves shared success by creating value for your customers and capturing value for your firm.

In the next chapter, we'll describe how several organizations used insights from customer chain analysis to succeed in their markets.

Figure 2.5: Complex Customer Chain Map

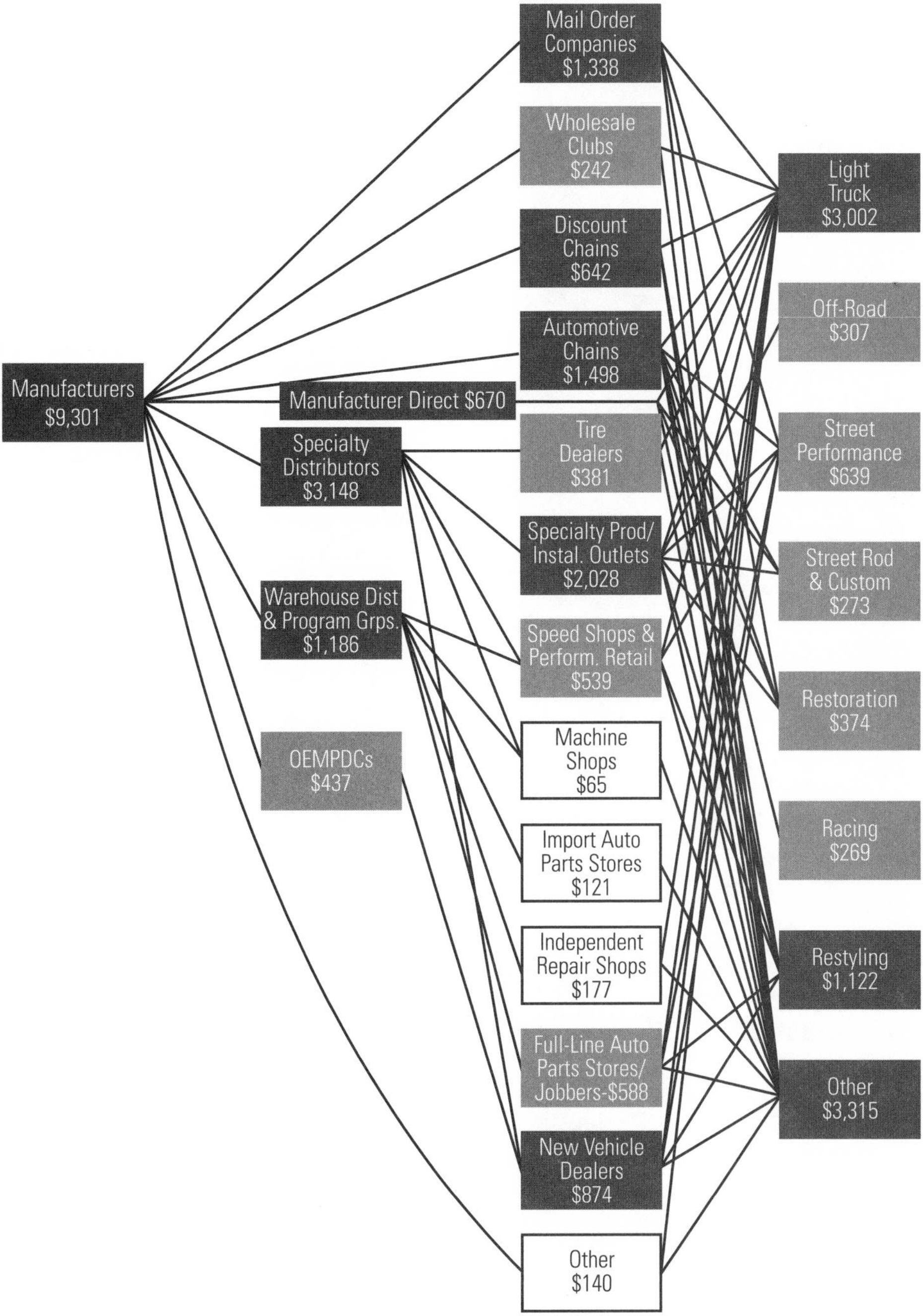

Chapter 3

SUCCESS STORIES: INSIGHTS FROM THE CUSTOMER CHAIN

Over the years, we've heard from thousands of business leaders about their successful growth as they've created value by analyzing their customer chains. These success stories involve industries from A to Z, spanning almost every imaginable product and service. They've taken place in developed markets and emerging markets alike, affected both small and large firms, and occurred in the context of major and minor business relationships.

INSIGHTS FROM LATER-STAGE CUSTOMERS

A recent analysis of these success stories revealed the most common ways that companies create and capture value through their customer chains. Many companies found success by focusing on later-stage customers, those somewhat further along the customer chain from their own firm.

Emerson looked to its later-stage customers when it addressed contractors' problems with installing water heaters. In that instance, there was no reason whatsoever for this supplier to link the installation problems to the components it manufactured. But as the problem was uncovered and understood, our client was able to implement a product enhancement that detected an improper installation and signaled the installer to that effect. The story ended in success because Emerson placed a high value on insights into how every participant along the customer chain interacted with its products.

A similar success story involved an electrical equipment manufacturer that sold its products through a network of distributors. The end customers were contractors who worked for a variety of commercial and industrial firms. Following the traditional work process, the contractors bought the necessary parts from a distributor and assembled them on-site. Our research, however, revealed that this step added substantially to the overall time required to complete a construction project; delays were blamed on a range of reasons, from adverse weather to failure to obtain the necessary parts from the distributor. This process was only a small part of their overall effort, but because it could delay all other activities if not completed promptly, contractors were not pleased with the product offering.

As it gained insights about these later-stage customers, the manufacturer identified the opportunity to create a solution that these customers would value: Get specs from a contractor, build the subsystem in the factory, and ship it to the work site, ready for installation. The firm tested this concept with contractors, experienced tremendous approval, and implemented the processes necessary to make it workable. These processes required substantial changes in how the three customer chain participants interacted. Distributors, for example, had to generate specs from their contractor customers, but would no longer hold inventory or touch the product at any point. The success story was enjoyed all along the customer chain: The contractors eliminated a troublesome problem and improved their own efficiency and on-time performance, gaining a competitive advantage in the process. The distributors and electrical manufacturer saw their products gain favor with contractors over their competitors' more traditional offerings.

One engine manufacturer whose products were sold on agricultural equipment saw sales growth in China and asked us to conduct end customer research. When the Chinese farmers explained how they used the equipment in light of difficulties unique to their environment, the manufacturer was able to respond with solutions as simple as changing the instructions that accompanied the products. In another instance, a paint manufacturer showed its container supplier our research on consumer attitudes toward the product, including negative feedback about the simple tasks of opening and closing the paint cans. Together the firms were able to address the issue with a new design that was well received in the market.

Some of the most fascinating success stories come from supplier-customer teams that identify ways to help later-stage customers increase sales. One story involves a construction equipment manufacturer and its direct customers, the distributors carrying its product. Research indicated that the next-stage customers, the contracting firms that used the equipment, were purchasing other products and shifting to other outlets simply because they failed to understand recent enhancements made to the product in question. An outreach campaign, designed by the manufacturer and implemented by personnel from the major distributors, was able to educate the contractors about how these enhancements could improve their job performance. The result was a sharp uptick in sales as the contractors suddenly understood the value of the enhancements and took advantage of the equipment to achieve greater productivity.

A manufacturer that sells components of a power system in the telecommunications market offers a similar success story. The complex customer chain comprised multiple stages, ending with the telecom business units that installed the equipment and those that supervised its operation and maintenance. According to our research, the telecom procurement individuals who selected the equipment for this system had failed to consider the significant costs—labor, downtime, parts replacement—of frequent maintenance and repairs of the equipment and its components throughout the product's life cycle. As expected, the procurement function was interested only in the initial price and whether the products met the engineering specs for quality, reliability, and durability. Once the component supplier made a greater effort to educate its customer chain about the implications of the different purchase options, however, new perspectives prevailed at several stages of this complex customer chain. The component and equipment suppliers had a better product that effectively decreased phone outages and downtime. Both suppliers realized rewards from their contributions, which had helped the later-stage customers manage their life-cycle costs.

When a packaging manufacturer approached one of its major cosmetics industry customers with an idea for making its products really stand out in stores, one of the cosmetics executives was impressed:

In our business, the products have short life cycles. And it's deadly if the customer looks at the shelf and sees a tired old product. We had been working with this supplier for some time and had shared some concepts about merchandising with them. They came to us with an idea, something we had never thought of. It caught our attention, and both companies put some design people on it. Then we did some testing in the marketplace and worked together to solve a few manufacturing issues. The results have been spectacular. This product has already been in the market for more than twice as long as our normal cycles, and it is still going strong.

The packaging executive who was the driving force behind this initiative reflected on the insight that had started the process—when a retailer, many stages down the customer chain, bemoaned the short shelf life of these products.

Probably the most important lesson to take from these case studies is this: Every participant along the customer chain hears messages from these later-stage customers, and these messages are worth taking seriously. We worked with one supplier who explained the difference between the best customers and the most difficult ones: "The best customers help us gain access to end customers, to hear their issues and concerns, while our most difficult customers think it's their job to stand in the way, to create a barrier that keeps us away from the end customers." This business leader marveled at some of its customers, saying, "We've even been threatened by some customers with the loss of business if we try to talk to their customers. You'd think we were the enemy rather than a major supplier whose products make a difference to these end users." Unfortunately, our experience tells us that this outlook is all too common.

Our case studies have also taught us that an open mind is as important as open eyes and ears as business leaders look up and down the customer chain. There is no reason to restrict takeaway messages to those associated with product performance or problems. As the following stories illustrate, seemingly unrelated messages can trigger awareness of how a supplier-customer team can perform at a higher level.

One company has implemented what we characterize as a best-practice program of sharing, on an annual basis, its top business challenges with key supplier organizations. These challenges are presented by the firm's business unit leaders, supported by senior engineers, sales executives, and other appropriate functional groups. Each year's issues are chosen purely "because they are our top business challenges, not because we've tried to connect them to our supply chain"; in other words, the firm has no intention of finger-pointing. It merely believes that by openly confronting these priority issues and providing a genuine foundation of shared trials and mutual history, it increases the odds that someone from among these key supplier partners will bring ideas to the table that will address the challenge.

INSIGHTS FROM RESTRUCTURED CUSTOMER CHAINS

Other insights from the customer chain often come when the market is restructuring or undergoing consolidation and other change. We've used insights into customer chain structures to help clients manage many of their decisions about how to address these changes. For example, we've learned that the success of an acquisition or merger depends not only on the two firms involved in the transaction, but also on decisions made by other participants along the firms' respective customer chains.[3]

The figure below reflects the major elements of the customer chain in a high-technology industry. The key participants in this market included four major manufacturers with competing product lines, three large wholesaler organizations, two large firms that provided technology integration services, and five distinct end customer segments. Figure 3.1 shows the principal linkages among these organizations.

Figure 3.1: High-technology Product Customer Chain Map

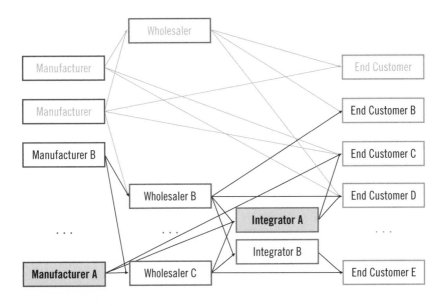

---

3. See Atlee Valentine Pope, David G. Hartman, Jon T. Gabrielsen, and George F. Brown, Jr., *Creating—Rather than Destroying—Value through Acquisitions* (Evanston, IL: Blue Canyon Partners, Inc., 2008).

One of the manufacturers (Manufacturer A, represented by the shaded box) acquired an integrator (Integrator A, reflected by the shaded box) at the third stage of this customer chain structure. It did so in order to improve its ability to provide solutions and to bring higher-value services to its customers. With this effort, it hoped to differentiate itself from its competitors. As the figure shows, these two organizations had been linked in the past, and the marketplace successes they had enjoyed together gave them confidence in the move.

Customer chain issues began to surface, however, as these newly combined organizations worked to implement a growth strategy. For example, one of the other manufacturers, Manufacturer B, was concerned about compromising its competitive position; it told its Wholesalers B and C to stop shipments to Integrator A. This led to a significant issue with Integrator A's major end customer, End Customer C, which had a strong preference for Manufacturer B's products and was unwilling to shift to new products, given its large installed base of equipment using Manufacturer B's products. So the acquired company, Integrator A, lost that major end customer's business as a result of its stronger association with the competing manufacturer.

In a second example, the acquiring company, Manufacturer A, tried to convert End Customer E from a competitor to the newly acquired Integrator A. Manufacturer A's products were already in use by this end customer, and it made a pitch reflecting the benefits of the improved solutions now available through Integrator A. In this case, the end customer's loyalty was far stronger to the competing Integrator B than to Manufacturer A; it stayed with Integrator B even through a shift to Manufacturer B's products, believing that it "could no longer trust Manufacturer A given the attempts to pirate our business and give it to Integrator A."

The message here: The driving rationale of this acquisition was sound along many dimensions, but the customer chain issues were so significant that the two organizations, according to a senior executive, "spent the first two years just getting back to the starting line, with no time available for any real focus on the underlying concept of delivering high-value solutions."

INSIGHTS INTO CHANGING ROLES
ALONG THE CUSTOMER CHAIN

One client was a distributor that had grown through acquisition, successfully moving into new regions by acquiring a niche distributor to serve those markets and then integrating that acquisition into the parent company's superior business and logistics systems. One of these regional acquisitions had previously acquired a small manufacturing firm, which it used to make private-label products to be sold under this smaller distributor's brand. After the acquisition, the parent distributor moved this private-label offering into its own catalog, branding it under the parent distributor's name and making it available to its wider customer base.

The reaction from some of this distributor's suppliers was swift and angry; they viewed this move as a breach of faith and began positioning the distributor as a competitor rather than as a business partner. One supplier asked, "Why would we want to use our brand to attract customers to this distributor, knowing that they'll pitch the benefits of their own house brand over ours?" This supplier substantially reduced the number of units that it was willing to sell through the distributor, and it began to favor other distributors for new product releases and programs designed to generate demand. While this reaction was extreme, other suppliers also factored the introduction of the private-label brand into their calculations and negotiations with the distributor.

Insights based on the customer chain—and on the organization's understanding of that structure—can not only define future success stories involving value creation, but also help to spotlight problems that arise when decisions might disrupt existing customer relationships. As we proceed to develop other elements of our methodology, we'll see how alignment with promising customer chains is the best way to begin creating value.

Chapter 4

ALIGN YOUR BUSINESS WITH WINNING CUSTOMER CHAINS

Once your company has *defined* its various customer chains, the next step toward creating and capturing value is to pick the *winning* customer chains. Typically, you'll recognize them by the strength of their participants. Firms that want to solve their growth challenges by creating value for their customers and capturing value for themselves will typically find it easier to do so if the other participants along the customer chain are also well positioned to accomplish this task. You can single out the winning customer chain in your market by locating the participants who are best positioned to respond successfully and consistently to a variety of business challenges.

As we began our work with one organization, its leaders started the conversation by admitting that they didn't know whether the future would bring success or failure to their business. The only thing they were sure of was uncertainty and change.

They went on to describe four fundamental changes taking place in their business environment. First, they recognized that new environmental regulations were in place and would begin to be enforced in the near future. Second, they identified changes in smart technology that would incorporate new, real-time information and control capabilities into certain product lines. Third, the firm's leaders cited significant industry consolidation at one stage of the customer chain, as large national participants at that stage rolled up small, local firms. And finally, this firm had identified an emerging e-channel that in less than two years had gone from no market share whatsoever to a high-single-digit share.

Together with this firm, we developed a detailed Customer Chain Map of the market environment in which it operated along with its competitors. We identified twenty-two distinct customer chain structures of consequence, some of them involving as many as six stages. About 80 percent of the firm's revenues fell within six of the customer chain structures, and the remaining 20 percent spanned another six structures. There were ten customer chain structures in which this firm didn't participate, for a variety of reasons.

Creating the Customer Chain Map enabled us to systematically assess the implications of the changes occurring in this market. Figure 4.1 provides an extract from that assessment, for ten of the twenty-two customer chain structures.

Using the Customer Chain Map and the insights about each of the twenty-two structures within it, including the newly emerging e-channel customer chain, we did an evaluation of the changes in each category and their likely impact on each customer chain structure. Our assessment system used codes that range from ++ (the change favored that customer chain structure) through -- (the change was likely to threaten that customer chain structure). These coded rankings are shown in the table.

Figure 4.1: Assessing Changes That Will Impact Ten Customer Chains

	Environ-mental Changes	Technology Changes	Industry Consolida-tion	New e-Channel	Summary
Customer Chain 1	++	+	++		+
Customer Chain 2		+		-	
Customer Chain 3	+	++	+		+
Customer Chain 4	--		-	--	-
Customer Chain 5	-	-	--	-	-
Customer Chain 6		--			
Customer Chain 7	++	+	+		+
Customer Chain 8		-	-	--	-
Customer Chain 9	+	++	+		+
"e" Customer Chain			+	++	+

Key: ++ very favorable, + favorable, - somewhat threatening, -- very threatening

The first six customer chains shown in the table above accounted for the bulk of this firm's business. Among them were two customer chain structures (customer chains 1 and 3) whose prospects seemed to be enhanced by the changes taking place, two whose prospects seemed to be threatened (customer chains 4 and 5), and two where the impact seemed to be modest (customer chains 2 and 6). These results provided the basis for a number of significant strategic decisions, spotlighting where and how to "double up on bets" and where to redirect business from endangered customer chains. Taken together, these plans of action enabled the firm to work from the strength of its legacy business while positioning itself for success in growth segments and incorporating plans to manage problems in other segments.

The assessment of the other sixteen customer chain structures was just as important. Two emerged with very favorable outlooks, while one of the smaller structures had an outlook that was among the most unfavorable. The assessment of the new e-channel reinforced the firm's speculation that its future was positive; some factors worked in support of that channel, and none were deemed likely to undermine it. As a result, this firm put into place action plans to enter the three new customer chains projected to be future winners, as well as plans to avoid losses in the one problematic smaller channel.

While this evaluation didn't provide the firm with explicit instructions on how best to create value, it drew attention to the customer chains where the firm's attempts to create value were most likely to yield a payoff in terms of growth. Combined, the plans to sustain business in the six traditional customer chains and to enter the three new structures created a bright outlook in terms of new business for this firm.

Sometimes, a changing business environment forces a company to realign with existing customer chains. Figure 4.2a reflects the many customer chain structures in place when we first worked with one component supplier in a complex high-technology business market.

As the first three rows of the figure suggest, our client faces two significant competitors (Component Supplier X and Component Supplier Y) whose product lines parallel its own in terms of breadth and depth; variations do exist in technology, quality, and price points, however. All three suppliers sell principally to three original equipment manufacturers (OEMs A, B, and C). As suggested in the first row, our

Figure 4.2a: Component Supplier Customer Chain Map

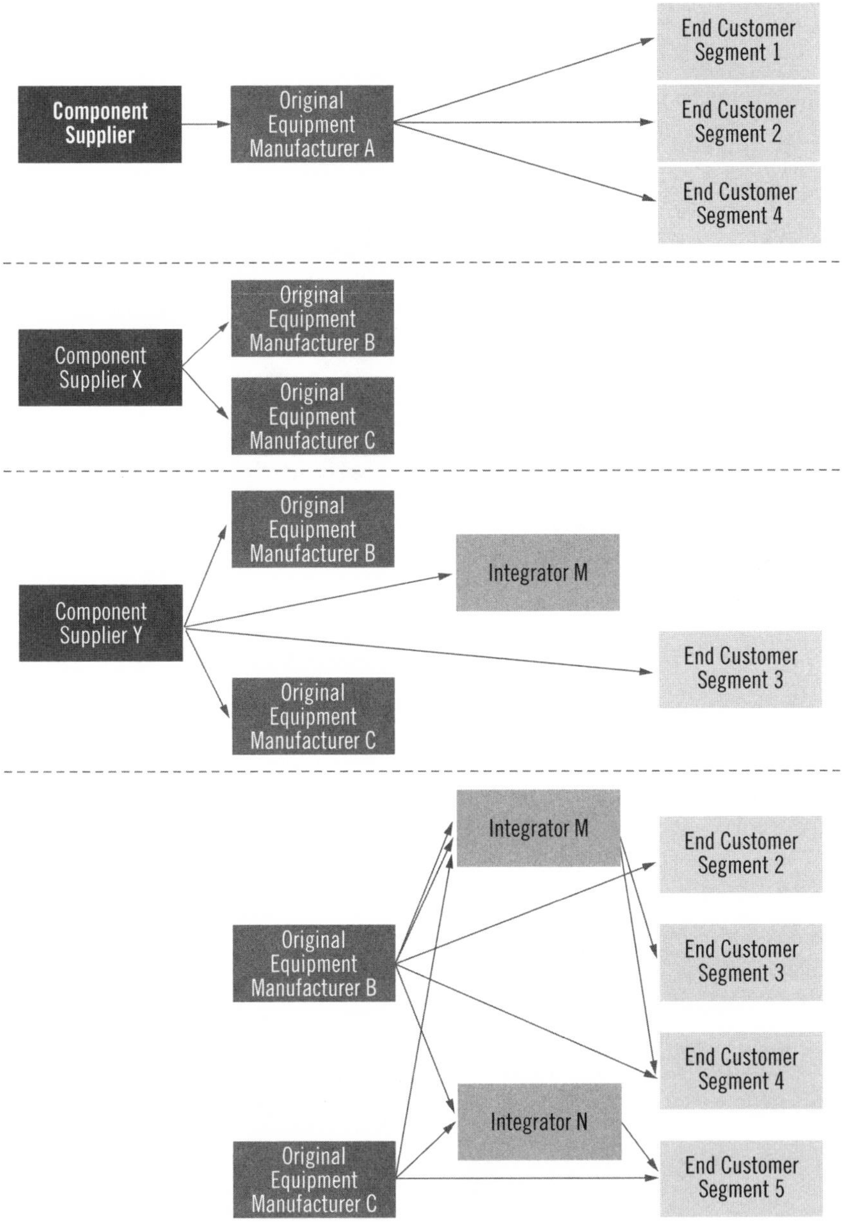

client sells directly to OEM A, who in turn reaches three end customer segments, End Customer Segment 1, End Customer Segment 2, and End Customer Segment 4. Component Supplier Y sells to two equipment manufacturers but also has direct relationships with Integrator M and End Customer Segment 3 (as shown in the third row). The final row of figure 4.2a illustrates that End Customer Segments 2 through 5 are supplied by a mix of OEM B and OEM C as well as through the two Integrators. The entire complexity of all these interrelationships is shown in figure 4.2b.

Our client had developed a close relationship with OEM A, and its ingredient brand had become an important part of this OEM's own positioning. This component supplier's ingredient had a dominant position in End Customer Segment 1, a leading position in End Customer Segment 2, and a small share in End Customer Segment 4. In all three

Figure 4.2b: Component Supplier Customer Chain Map

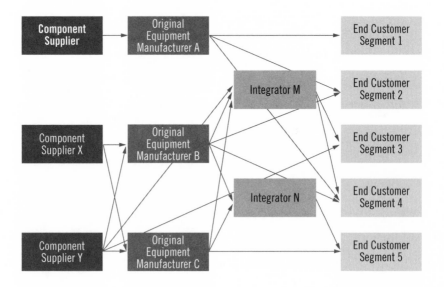

of these segments, this supplier and its OEM partner were successful because they offered a solid, reliable product at a price point significantly lower than that of their competitors. But the supplier's most important success came from its focus on End Customer Segment 1. In the two years after it implemented its growth strategy, the supplier grew by five percentage points faster than the rest of the market. So by understanding the customer chain, our client was able to benefit from the growth of certain market segments as well as increase its market share.

When this firm began to see its markets soften in early 2000, its leaders asked us to revisit their strategy and help them align with winning customer chains. Across the three end markets most important to this firm and its OEM partner, the outlook and opportunities were quite different. In End Customer Segment 1, prospects were better than average; since our client already held a strong position as a result of its price leadership, challenges from competitors were unlikely in that market. End Customer Segment 2, on the other hand, was projected to be under considerable pressure as the economy worsened. By targeting that segment and working closely with its OEM partner (OEM A) to improve service capabilities at a more competitive price point, this supplier was able to pick up share in that market segment.

End Customer Segment 4 presented a distinct opportunity. The competing customer chains were all positioned at a relatively high price point, with Integrator M under extreme pressure, burdened by high product costs. This integrator struggled to justify the value of its professional services to end customers who were facing considerable budgetary pressure. In response to these pressures, our client and OEM A created a new customer chain relationship with Integrator M to serve End Customer Segment 4, providing the integrator with a *better* option at a lower price to augment the traditional *best* offering it already had in the market. As a result, our client's sales in this segment, although small to begin with, nearly doubled despite the downturn.

From this case study and others, we've developed three important guidelines for organizations that seek to sustain and grow their business by aligning with the other participants in winning customer chains.

1. **Understand the customer chain segments.** The first guideline emphasizes the importance of understanding the customer chain segments within the target market, each of which is likely to be distinct in terms of structure, economics, critical success factors, and competition. In the case study above, the economics remained relatively favorable for End Customer Segment 1 during the downturn, and nothing took place to significantly shift decision drivers or the competitive balance. In contrast, the external environment was materially reshaping business priorities in End Customer Segments 2 and 4, creating an opening for the component supplier to exploit its price advantage. Finding winning customer chains and identifying ways to create value for their participants were the sources of success for this firm.

2. **Examine each stage of the customer chain.** Second, businesses must look at each and every stage of the customer chain in order to gain maximum insight. In the example above, the changes in purchase decisions were taking place not adjacent to the component supplier but several stages further along the customer chain. The insights that lead to eventual success did not center on the relationship between this supplier and its OEM partner but

rather on the later-stage firms served by this team. Our client's investment in understanding later-stage customer chain participants, such as the integrators and the end customers, provided the foundation necessary for taking early and appropriate actions.

3. **Create "win-win-win" outcomes for all customer chain participants.** The third guideline focuses on the need to develop successes among all the participants in your customer chains. In this particular case, the supplier and the OEM collaborated to implement action plans within all three customer chains. This was, admittedly, an exceptional working relationship. Nevertheless, the ability of two organizations to share information and swiftly agree on action plans reinforces the gains that come from best-in-class supplier-customer relationships like this one. But the benefits weren't just a two-way street; this supplier and its OEM partner in fact created a win-win-win outcome by bringing a solution to the pressures faced by the integrator, which also was able to realize success in a difficult market environment.

The approaches that business leaders take to identify opportunities for creating value are most likely to yield rewards when applied to healthy, growing customer chain structures. So by finding the winning customer chains, you can spotlight where resources can best be applied to the challenges of creating and capturing value. Once you identify the healthy customer chains that will applaud and use this value, the value itself will allow you to overcome your growth challenges. In the next chapter we will examine how to determine whether the aligned customer chain will, in fact, adopt these ideas and accept a co-destined relationship.

Chapter 5

CREATE VALUE FOR YOUR CUSTOMERS: THREE APPROACHES

Once your company has defined its customer chains and aligned itself properly with the winning participants, the real work of creating and capturing value begins. Each business along the customer chain looks back at its suppliers and forward at its markets to determine which decisions will result in continued growth and the strongest possible rewards for its own shareholders.

The economics of business markets builds upon this simple proposition, which defines our approach to value creation. For a supplier to command a higher price or to win a customer's business over its competition, the business customer must perceive that it will be better off buying from that supplier—and that it in fact prefers the supplier's higher-priced product. This matter-of-fact statement defines how business customers make decisions, and it creates a framework for identifying the ways in which a firm can create value for its customers.

What emerges from this framework is a powerful insight. It's actually saying that there are three ways—and only three ways—for a supplier to create value from the perspective of a potential business customer: *increase market share, increase prices,* or *cut costs.*

An organization can *increase market share* for a business customer if the customer believes it can increase its market share only by choosing the supplier's product—even at a higher price. Perhaps customers further along the customer chain favor the supplier's ingredient, motivating them to purchase products that incorporate that ingredient. Or maybe a distributor believes it can use a particular supplier's product as a magnet for customers who may go on to purchase additional products from the catalog. We've also seen situations where share gains have been linked to products that incorporate sustainable technology.

An organization can help *increase prices* for a business customer if the customer believes it can turn around and achieve a price premium for its own products—by passing along the higher price of the supplier's product to its own customers. The most obvious examples are firms that provide a spectrum of products with different ingredients, at different price points. Many commercial truck manufacturers offer additional options above and beyond the standard equipment, and, for components such as engines, transmissions, and axles, the higher-priced option often is the most popular. Customers are willing to pay for pricier products because they believe these purchases will save them money in the long term.

In both of these approaches to value creation, the supplier's direct customer must believe that its own customers will reward it—with either a share premium or a price premium (or both)—for incorporating the supplier's products or for offering the supplier's higher-priced products.

A supplier organization can *cut costs* for a business customer if that customer believes it can save money elsewhere in its business by selecting that supplier's product over the competition's or by trading up to the supplier's higher-priced product. This decision can be made entirely within the business customer's firm as part of its efforts to optimize its manufacturing processes, reduce the cost of warranty claims, lower the cost of providing any services that are linked to its products, or otherwise remove costs from the equation and thus improve its bottom line. In some cases, these savings might be passed along to shareholders in the form of higher profits. In other instances, they might be passed along to the firm's own customers via lower prices, strengthening the firm's own competitive position and increasing its market share.

Take note: We are not advocating that the supplier lower its prices. Price-based competition arises only when suppliers fail to introduce unique ways to create value for their customers. When competing suppliers haven't invested in some type of value that distinguishes their products, the business customer—forced to cut costs when it cannot pass on premium prices to the end customer—will demand lower prices in return for doing business with the supplier. In other words, this approach to creating value is a last resort. The supplier is saying to its customer, "There is nothing of value I can do for you, other than cutting my price."

Great opportunities for growth can emerge when a firm steps into its customers' shoes in order to understand what contributions it can make to strengthen its customers' own business performance. Successful business strategy can be built upon a detailed understanding of the customers' plans, pains, and priorities.

These win-win outcomes—where the supplier wins business and/or realizes higher prices while also giving the customer some sort of advantage—are at the economic heart of business-to-business relationships. Those suppliers who create value with a proposal that makes their customers better off in some way will be rewarded with higher margins, a stronger customer relationship, and profitable growth.

This model for value creation holds true for companies in any market. At a recent meeting with one of our clients, we gave the executive team a pop quiz. The instructions were to read the following success stories of three customers—about a supplier in a different industry—and characterize Supplier A.

Customer 1 said:

"We're in an industry defined by short product life cycles. If the customer looks at our offering and doesn't see anything new, that customer looks at our competitors instead. Supplier A came to us with an idea that would allow us to update the product as often as we wanted—the typical time required by our other suppliers to adjust to a new release would be reduced to next to nothing. We are always cited in surveys for new product innovation, and now our engineers can implement a modest upgrade without the organization having to jump through hoops. At this point, Supplier A is getting all our business."

Customer 2 said:

"We all had a lot at stake with this new product, and we were surprised when a performance issue surfaced. We had two suppliers at this point, and we expected Supplier B to say, "What can we do to help?" Instead they said, "We recommend that you go back to the drawing board." This was communicated at upper management levels first, which really wreaked havoc with our technical team. Money was on the table and careers were at stake—the supplier just didn't understand the seriousness of the situation. One of our engineers talked to Supplier A. It turned out that they had faced a very similar problem with a customer in Europe. They flew in two engineers who spent a month with us and got the problem resolved."

Customer 3 said:

"Supplier A brought a team to our organization, demonstrated a new approach, and showed us how we could eliminate a significant amount of materials—which we were buying from them, by the way—and eliminate two steps in the manufacturing process. It has saved us a lot of money."

The executives at this meeting concluded that the supplier being described was a high-technology firm, probably supplying the cell phone or computer market.

In fact, the company was a packaging supplier. Its products were, by the company's own description, "pretty darn basic"; its costs were measured in cents and fractions of cents. It did own a few patents, but by and large, its business was a commodity business. Nonetheless, its customers considered it to be a company that could bring substantial value into their relationships. The packaging supplier created value for its customer by increasing market share, increasing revenue, and cutting cost.

Innovation in packaging turned out to be a significant contributor to Customer 1's merchandising strategy; the supplier helped the customer establish its position as an innovator by constantly enhancing its product line. The packaging firm was able to eliminate a barrier to the customer's success; its near-instant ability to evolve the packaging in concert with the products' evolution led to faster product introduction. This type of contribution created value from Customer 1's perspective: The customer is selling a branded, differentiated product—and either getting a premium price or enjoying a substantial market share.

Many brands compete within customer chains involving tough end customers who demand the best. When end customers can choose from among many competing options, they'll always look for innovation, something new, a stand-out offering from the manufacturers and (further back along the customer chain) their suppliers. While the firm's product innovations were behind this success story, the packaging supplier's ability to keep pace with its customer's innovations was critical to marketplace success. Because its innovation created value, end customers were eager to pay more for a product that delivered more. The customer was able to increase its market share and its revenue, and the supplier reaped the rewards of the customer's continued business.

Customer 2 was able to resolve certain performance issues when its supplier sought to bring value to the relationship. Every business customer in every industry faces important technical challenges. Often, the end customer's purchase decisions depend upon the manufacturer's success in meeting these technical challenges, whether with product safety, performance, reliability, shelf life, or any other area that matters to the end customers. This is one of the ways the manufacturer can differentiate itself from its competition.

The problem faced by Customer 2 was one of product leakage,

with a host of bad implications, including significant returns, wastage, and overall dissatisfaction among its end customers. The cause of the problem was a change in the product's chemistry from the previous generation; the solution required only a modest change in the packaging materials and the filling process. The firm was able to launch its new product on time and, after a few tweaks to the process, at the targeted price point. Like Supplier A in this case, any firm in any industry can increase profitability if it can recognize the technical challenges facing its customers and provide solutions that create value in at least one of the three ways: by yielding improved market successes (reflected in either market share or prices) or by affecting operations in some way that translates into gains for the bottom line.

Bottom-line gains were the game changer for Customer 3. In this case, Supplier A created value for its customer by improving its processes and competitiveness, thus taking costs out of the system. These types of value contributions are often invisible to customers further along the customer chain, since they involve process changes, material substitutions, or shifts in the roles of the supplier and its direct customer as well as the boundaries between them. The supplier in this case study, understanding how its customer used its packaging to protect the product, reengineered its offering to achieve the same level of protection with a simpler packaging solution. As the example noted, this reduced the materials used, which created a short-term reduction in the supplier's sales to this customer—a route that many businesses might shy away from. But in our discussions, both this supplier and this customer noted that the contribution was "a great long-term business decision." This supplier's approach to its customer relationship was focused on helping its customer succeed, which would eventually result in future business awards and growth; there was never any question about whether it was appropriate to surface this innovation.

Now we've seen how any company can create value for its customers in three ways. An important part of that value creation process, however, involves matching opportunities to the right market segments. The next chapter describes an approach to market segmentation that your business can use to create value and capture these opportunities.

Chapter 6

SEGMENT YOUR CUSTOMERS BY THEIR PURCHASE BEHAVIORS

When companies segment their markets according to factors that drive buying behavior, they can identify how to create value and learn which obstacles must be overcome in their pursuit of sustainable growth. Our work with a capital equipment manufacturer serving industrial customers around the globe helped the firm rethink its approach to segmenting its market. This firm had invested in a segmentation study that categorized its markets, as described by one company leader, "eight ways from Sunday: by geographic region, by vertical industry, by size of the customer organization—by just about everything but the color of the CEO's eyes." The results were disappointing. The firm's leaders gained certain insights, but in retrospect, these findings weren't a whole lot better than learning that, say, tall men are more likely than shorter men to buy long sizes. As a result of the study, the firm put more sales resources into the segments where it had strong shares, thinking its value proposition was working there. Ultimately, however, it failed to gain much growth. Worse, these results also generated a horror story when the firm changed its strategy in one segment where it had a weak share—only to lose some of the few customers it had.

The manufacturing firm was battling with two niche competitors. Each of these three firms offered advanced technology and provided exceptional support to its respective customers. Our client had a far greater market share than the two niche firms, while those organizations' specialty offerings were uniquely matched to two vertical markets with unique requirements. There were also two major competitors in the industry, one a "solid Toyota to our Lexus, with good products at a fair price, but not at the edge in terms of technology or services," and the other described as the firm with "the bargain-basement offer, with very low-priced products, often using past-generation technology and with bare-bones support."

While the number of competitors and their positioning varies from industry to industry, we often hear descriptions such as these. The three major players serve markets segmented by buying behavior. The firm at the top end of the market serves those customers whose purchase decisions are driven by state-of-the-art technology and extensive support. The low-end firm focuses on those searching for the lowest possible prices. The middle-of-the-road firm reaches customers whose priorities involve a balance between product features and price. For these three firms, segmentation efforts are valuable to the extent that they cluster customers by purchase decisions. Segmentation by geographic region or vertical industry or other demographic factors, on the other hand, is relevant only when there is a strong overlap in customer buying behavior. Our client's disappointment in the earlier study was justified—the study hadn't reflected this insight regarding purchase decisions. It hadn't taken into account the high-end customers, middle-of-the-road customers, and price buyers in essentially every vertical or geographic market segment that was researched.

We've learned that the greatest insights—those that lead to an understanding of how a firm can create value for customers and grow with them—come when business leaders segment markets not on demographics but on the factors that drive purchase decisions. It's not that customer demographics are unimportant; even in this example, studying customer demographics is quite a good starting point for the two niche firms with concentrations in specific vertical markets. But in general, for a company that seeks to identify growth markets and develop strategies for creating value, segmentation on buying behavior is critical to success.

Our research has defined a process for segmenting markets on the basis of buying behavior.[4] The process starts when we define the customer chain structures that exist within the market. We take pains to understand the behavior of each and every participant along the customer chain. Frequently, the key factors that drive decisions vary from one stage of the customer chain to the next. In fact, we've come to observe that understanding the *horizontal* pathway of purchase decisions along the customer chain is far more insightful than studying the profile and demographics of the *vertical* end customer markets.

Numerous factors enter into the purchase decisions of each participant in the customer chain. Buying behavior can be shaped by economics in subsequent stages—reflected in, for example, the elasticity of demand. If one business customer faces end customers whose

4. See Atlee Valentine Pope and George F. Brown, Jr., *A Blueprint for Success with Major Customers* (Evanston, IL: Blue Canyon Partners, Inc., 1998). See also George F. Brown, Jr., and David G. Hartman, *Business-to-Business Economics* (Evanston, IL: Blue Canyon Partners, Inc., 2006).

purchases shift significantly in response to modest price changes, that firm would weigh the impact of supplier prices more heavily than would a direct customer whose market segment is less reactive to price changes. Similarly, a direct customer is likely to focus more intensely on the price of a significant ingredient in its products than on the price of a minor ingredient. Visibility of the supplier's product to the end customer, the goals of purchasing managers, the degree of margin pressures faced by an organization, linkage of a product to the overall portfolio bought (or sold)—all these factors (and more) determine buying behavior.

One helpful tool in deciphering buyer behavior is our Market Map (figure 6.1), a graphical display of purchase decision drivers within a given market. The vertical axis of the map depicts the direct customer's purchase decisions, while the horizontal axis depicts the end customer's purchase decisions. The scale of each axis ranges from purchase decisions based on factors other than price to those based mostly on price. Breaking this map into four quadrants gives us a general understanding of the most important characteristics of these customers' decision drivers.

We've placed a bubble on this map to represent each particular customer chain and what drives its purchase decisions. If a customer chain falls in the lower left quadrant, the direct customer not only serves end customers who purchase based on non-price factors (such as product features and superior service), but also bases its own purchase decisions on factors other than suppliers' prices. If a customer chain falls in the lower right quadrant, the direct customer competes for the end customer's purchase on the basis of price; in this market, direct customers experience little price flexibility from their end customers. However,

Figure 6.1: Market Map

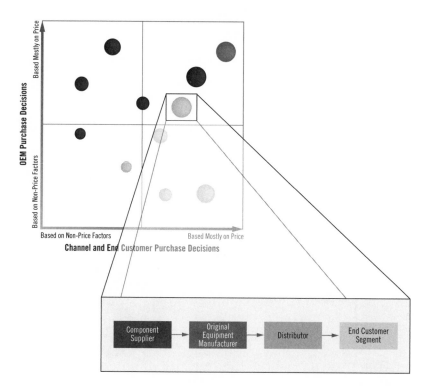

for various reasons, the direct customer's decisions for purchasing from its suppliers are still based on other factors. A supplier's offering might be only a small portion of the direct customer's overall costs or, on the contrary, might be pivotal and strategic to the customer (that is, the value it provides is more important than the cost).

If a customer chain falls in the upper left quadrant, end customers base their valuation of the direct customer's offer on factors other than price—they are looking for innovation and whatever may differentiate this product from competitors—while the direct customer considers price to be a significant factor, often because the supplier's product represents a significant portion of the direct customer's final offering. If a customer chain falls in the upper right quadrant, the direct customer and the end customer are both in extremely price-sensitive markets and will need the cooperation of suppliers to compete.

Let's examine some of the customer chains we've already discussed in order to demonstrate the utility of the Market Map.

The Emerson case study in chapter 1 revealed several distinct segments of the market for water heaters. The various drivers of purchase decisions about water heaters are reflected in figure 6.2.

Figure 6.2: Water Heater Market Map

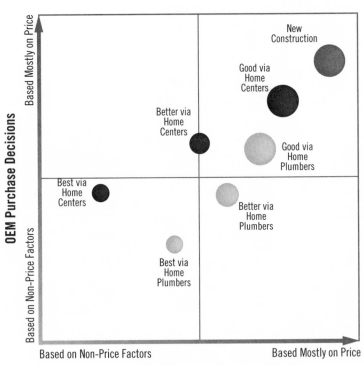

Channel and End Customer Purchase Decisions

While price was an important factor in many market segments, in Best segments, served by both the home center and the plumbing channels, factors other than price were the true drivers of purchase decisions at each stage of the customer chain. Best segments in this case involve high-end appliances with superior features and dependable installation service capabilities.

Similar findings emerged for the other product lines studied during this project. There were segments that reflected virtually every combination of purchasing behaviors—in some, price was critical, while product features and services were the critical factors in other segments. For example, water heaters sold to the home builder and installed by the plumbing contractor are represented by the New Construction bubble located in the upper right quadrant. In this customer chain, home builders are extremely cost conscious, operating on tight budgets and time frames. They know that homebuyers are far more interested in kitchen appliances and countertops; they are willing to spend money on these options and will try to save on water heaters instead. On the other hand, when end customers in the lower left quadrant experience a failed water heater in their homes, the plumber they call to quickly install the replacement is often able to upsell with best features such as faster heating and a warranty to cover labor on future service calls.

It is a rare market in which the segments are tightly clustered, all focused on the same factors in their purchase decision making. Instead, market bubbles are commonly scattered according to a variety of customer requirements and behaviors. The strategy that will yield success in each business environment differs considerably. The Market Map allows business leaders to segment markets on the basis of these business environments, providing crucial insight. Figure 6.3 summarizes the strategies most likely to yield success in each of the four business-to-business environments.

Figure 6.3: Market Map Strategies

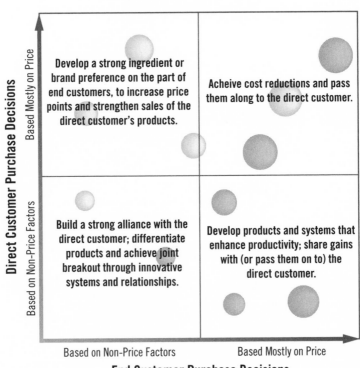

In the previous chapter, we described the three ways a supplier can create value for its customers—by enabling them to gain market share, to command premium prices, or to remove costs from their operations. To some extent, all these options are available in every business-to-business market. But certain factors—such as the characteristics of end customers, the priorities that exist for a specific direct customer, the nature of the direct customer's production processes and materials, and various competitive factors—play a role in defining the best way to create value for each customer chain segment.

We worked with one building systems manufacturer that served a number of distinct markets, through customer chains that hosted a combination of distributors, contractors, installers, and a variety of end customers. The factors that drove purchase decisions varied considerably across the customer chains within this company's markets. The Market Map for this building systems manufacturer is represented in figure 6.4.

Figure 6.4: Building Systems Market Map

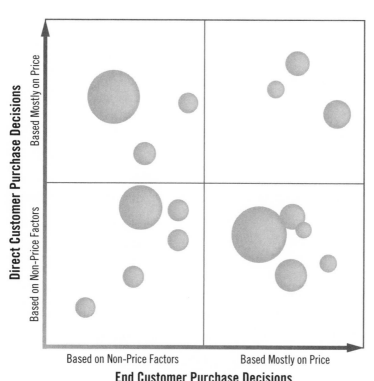

Direct Customer Purchase Decisions

Based Mostly on Price

Based on Non-Price Factors

Based on Non-Price Factors   Based Mostly on Price

End Customer Purchase Decisions

The segments in the lower right quadrant typically involved contractors and installers. While these businesses faced intensive competition from others in their local markets, their cost structure was dominated by labor—so anything that simplified the installation and saved time was of significant value. When our client's engineers redesigned equipment to dramatically simplify the installation process, the ultimate savings for the contractor—several stages along the customer chain—were significant. This gave a significant advantage to our client among these critical decision makers.

In the upper left quadrant, the end customer's focus is on the features, enhancements, and services offered by the direct customer's product; this means the supplier, by bringing innovation to the table, has an opportunity to help the direct customer differentiate its product. Direct customers facing profit challenges in this environment are forced to implement aggressive strategies to manage their supply chain. This creates a hurdle for the supplier. Yet it also underscores an opportunity for the supplier to make its ingredients visible to—and valued by—the end customers as well as the direct customer's marketing and design managers. So for customer chain segments within this environment, brand initiatives are critical to creating differentiation in products and services. One such example is the "Intel Inside" campaign. Supplier strategies that focus on gaining a share premium are the most likely to be effective; the customer's intense focus on supply chain management could create conflict if the supplier attempts to parlay end customers' preferences into too large of a price premium. (In chapter 7, we'll discuss strategies a supplier can use to establish a position with customers at later stages of the customer chain, and thereby drive success even when its direct customers are reticent about embracing its value contributions.)

Another client, an organization in the commercial vehicles market, operated alongside several well-aligned customer chain segments, with direct customers (e.g., truck manufacturers) and end customers (e.g., fleets) both focused on either superior operating characteristics (figure 6.5, lower left quadrant) or price (upper right quadrant). In several important segments, however, the manufacturers attempted to run aggressive bid competitions among suppliers, despite the fact that the

Figure 6.5: Commercial Vehicle Systems Market Map

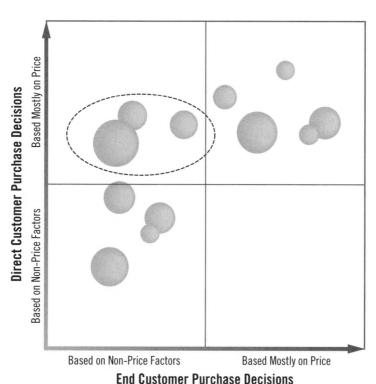

fleets purchasing their equipment were not particularly focused on price. These segments fell within the upper left quadrant in figure 6.5.

Our research on purchasing behavior spotlighted the fact that these fleets were sharp-penciled businesses, able to precisely calculate the positive impact (in terms of such factors as fuel economy and maintenance) of superior vehicle systems on their total cost of ownership. The supplier began to develop strong messages for the end customer organizations about the track record of its components in terms of total cost of ownership. The consequence of this newfound brand awareness was strong pull-through demand: Fleets began to specify that the vehicles they purchased be equipped with the supplier's superior-performing components.

The business environment represented in the lower left quadrant offers many opportunities for value creation. The supplier can create and capture value through ingredients that are valued by end customers, much as was the case in the upper left quadrant, with our client in the commercial vehicles market. But in this case the supplier can also implement innovations that improve market share and drive volume, much like the appropriate strategy for the lower right quadrant. And both of these efforts are more easily implemented in this lower-left-quadrant business environment, as the supplier will face neither the intense supply chain pressures of the upper left quadrant nor the price demands of the end customer in the lower right quadrant. This lower-left-quadrant business environment is often the laboratory in which good ideas are most easily incubated, brought to customers, and translated into joint wins. Successes with customers in this environment tend to be "reference successes"—those that help establish a supplier's leadership position.

The supplier in this environment has a clear-cut opportunity to move into a higher-level relationship with its direct customers. (In chapter 8, we'll talk about ways for businesses to create a Relationship Advantage with key customers and channel partners in order to introduce their contributions to value creation.) Freedom from overwhelming cost concerns means that the potential exists for the breakout of new concepts and product innovations. Supplier-customer alliances can put into place programs that not only ensure market leadership, but also steadily widen the gap between the supplier-customer team and its competitors. Suppliers in this environment are the most likely to realize a price premium; they're also more likely to share these premiums with the direct customer. Both partners can reap the rewards of their successful efforts to remove costs from the linked supplier-customer business systems.

One case study with segments in this business environment involved Snap-on Tools, a major supplier to the automotive service and other industries.[5] This company and its competitors served market segments that displayed price-based buying behavior (shown in the upper right quadrant, figure 6.6), as well as markets that offered opportunities for bringing high-value service and productivity to direct customers (shown in the lower right quadrant). There were also some significant segments in the lower left quadrant.

Snap-on Tools identified a number of specific product and service offerings that were viewed as important by the automotive technicians segment in that business environment. It developed a design strategy that "raised the bar" relative to the previous products that Snap-on

---

5. Michael G. Gentile, "Managing Brand and Channel Strategy" (Institute for the Study of Business Markets, November 2000).

Figure 6.6: Snap-on Tools Market Map

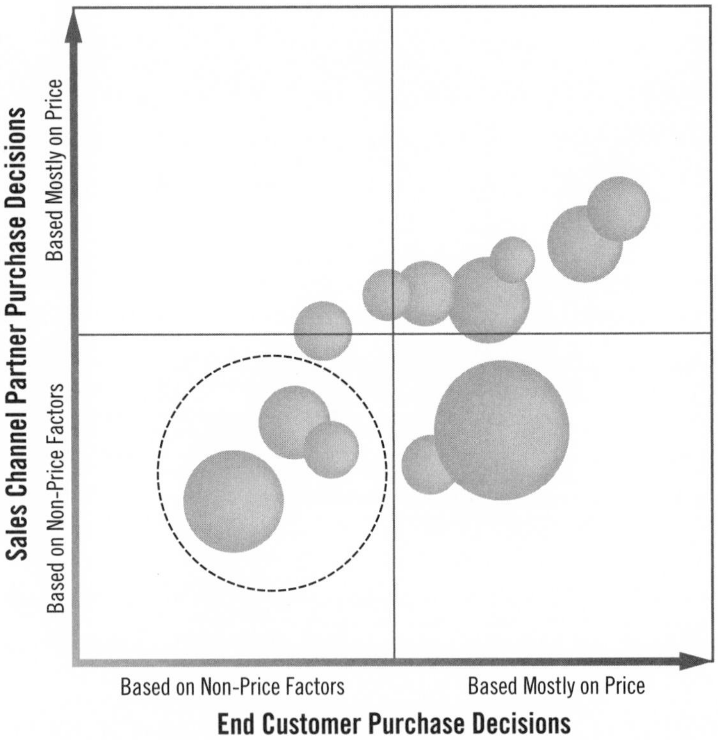
Sales Channel Partner Purchase Decisions
Based Mostly on Price
Based on Non-Price Factors
Based on Non-Price Factors
Based Mostly on Price
End Customer Purchase Decisions

and its competitors had taken to the market. Many of the product features targeted at this segment would have been viewed as unnecessary "bells and whistles" in other quadrants. Because it was familiar with the Market Map, however, the supplier had made brand structure and business relationship decisions that were correctly targeted toward the right customers and prospects.

The prescriptions for success differ considerably across the four business-to-business environments. The various strategies reflect the possible ways in which the supplier's contributions can connect to the factors that drive customer purchasing behavior. Except in the upper right quadrant, where only cost advantages are likely to lead to success, each business environment suggests ways for the supplier to grow. The supplier can create and capture value by connecting with the right decision-shaping priorities for each customer.

The environment in the lower right quadrant in particular opens the door for a supplier to contribute ideas that remove costs from the equation—in part because the supplier's product often plays a relatively modest role in the direct customer's cost and pricing structure. This matches well with the opportunity to increase value—in the form of productivity—for the direct customer through service strategies,[6] support with expanding the business globally,[7] or other approaches. In this business environment, suppliers should focus their strategies on eliminating costs for their direct customers. Ways to achieve this include productivity enhancements; changes in the roles performed by, and the functional boundaries between, supplier and customer; or other innovations that bring solutions to the direct customer.

When purchasing behavior is understood, it can be used as a basis for segmentation efforts that are worthwhile. It is then possible for business-to-business firms to match strategy choices to the factors that are important to the customers in each segment. Product lines and service offerings designed for particular segments can be matched to the potential for value creation for these customers, leading to previously untapped growth opportunities. Sales models and channel partner relationships can be structured to complement the

---

6. Atlee Valentine Pope and George F. Brown, Jr., "eSAM: Creating the 'e' Footprint for Strategic Accounts," *Velocity* (Winter 2001).
7. Atlee Valentine Pope and George F. Brown, Jr., "Three C's of Global Account Management," *Velocity* (Summer 1999).

product and service offerings. Pricing structures can be developed in a systematic fashion that yields rewards for shareholders while still meeting customers' needs. The lesson of segmenting on the basis of purchase decision factors is one that leads to winning choices. By matching its strategy for value creation to its market messages and economic structures, a firm can discern which customers to target, and how, in its quest to achieve the elusive win-win-win outcome.

Chapter 7

APPLY YOUR VALUE LEVERS: FROM VALUE CREATION TO VALUE CAPTURE

Business leaders study behavioral segmentation of their markets, as introduced in the previous chapter, to spotlight what creates value for customers at each stage of the customer chain—what meets their customers' specific unmet needs. By translating these insights into action plans that *respond* to those unmet needs, business leaders can capture value for their own shareholders. Indirectly, it is the customers who write a supplier's plans for value creation, according to their own requirements; they are selfishly thinking about how the supplier can better serve them. And yet this topsy-turvy system brings great benefit to the supplier.

In this chapter, we examine how a supplier can use its own influence: by developing, prioritizing, and manipulating value levers. *Value levers* are concrete actions that, if implemented, will resonate with customers, creating and capturing value along the customer chain. Value levers come in many different forms, from product innovations to new services to price changes to relationship enhancements. A supplier may be able to identify many different value levers based on messages and economic insights gleaned from customers up and down the customer chain. To ensure success, however, suppliers must choose the best levers to pull in order to create value. Some value levers are easier or quicker to pull than others, some are more inviting, and some fit better with the supplier's current business capabilities. As an organization determines which value lever to pull, its leaders must be confident that, ultimately, the chosen lever meets one or more of the three approaches to value creation described in chapter 5. That is, the value lever must increase market share, increase prices, and/or cut costs for the customer.

When a supplier chooses to implement the value lever, it then has an opportunity to capture for itself a portion of the value it is creating for its customers. This opportunity often correlates closely with the three approaches to value creation. When a supplier takes action to *create value* for its customer by helping its customer *increase market share,* the supplier is able to *capture value* by increasing its own volume and share of business with the customer. Suppliers that are able to help their customers *increase prices* can capture value from the customer with a price premium—the customer will accept a higher price from the supplier in return for helping the customer better its performance. And finally, if a supplier can help the customer *cut costs,* it can capture the value from this action by winning a greater share of the customer's business and/or by increasing its own prices when the customer agrees to pass along some of these savings to the supplier.

This concept goes to the very basis of the principle: In order to create value and then capture value, both the supplier and the customer must be better off. It has to be a win–win situation.

A leading packaging supplier found itself in a situation that illustrates the concept of creating and capturing value by using value levers.

This packaging supplier served a number of direct customers, including foodservice distributors, stand-alone and chain restaurants, fast-food chains, grocery stores, hospitality organizations, and cafeterias that served captive customer bases in facilities like hospitals and schools. These direct customers, in turn, served certain end customers, as suggested by the Customer Chain Map below (figure 7.1). The supplier's product line was comprehensive, including simple items such as paper and plastic bags, the packaging used for meats and vegetables, and the takeout packaging used by restaurants and fast-food chains.

Figure 7.1: Food Packaging Supplier Customer Chain Map

As we analyzed the economics of this market and spoke to its participants about the factors that drive purchase decisions, we found that the various customer chains fell within all four quadrants of our Market Map. What follows is our analysis of these segments, drawing on our study of buying behavior to identify which value levers this supplier should pull to activate value creation and value capture.

SERVING PRICE-SENSITIVE SEGMENTS

Some customer chains served by this packaging supplier violated our general belief that "customers want more—and they will pay for it." In the highly competitive grocery business, both the direct customers (the grocery stores) and the end customers (the consumers) focused almost exclusively on price—and told us so in no uncertain terms.

Figure 7.2: Grocery Takeout Food Packaging Customer Chain: Market Perceptions

Supplier	Grocery Store	Consumer
	Market Perceptions: • "This is an intensely competitive market. We have to meet market prices or lose the customer." • "No one is going to pay more for groceries because of the bag they come in." • "Customers just want the basic product at a low price."	**Market Perceptions:** • "We watch prices very carefully through the ads and T.V." • "No store is going to be able to charge more than the others." • "Most grocery products have been around for as long as I've been alive. They are basic products available everywhere."

When we asked customer chain participants to identify possible value levers, once again their answers focused on price.

Figure 7.3: Grocery Takeout Food Packaging Customer Chain: Needs

Supplier	Grocery Store	Consumer
	Needs: • "Give me low prices, quantity discounts, and most-favored-customer pricing." • "I'd like 'one size fits all,' which would mean lower inventories." • "Steady price reductions."	**Needs:** • "I'm not buying a bag—it's just something that the store uses to help me get my purchase home." • "All I want is a bag that does what it's supposed to do—not rip before I get home."

According to the Market Map, these segments were located in the upper right quadrant, with both the direct customers and the end customers focused mostly on price in their purchase decisions. What did we learn from these segments? Other than cost reductions, there

Figure 7.4: Market Map: Grocery Takeout Food Packaging

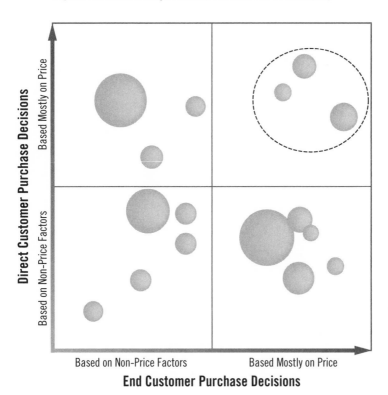

were very few value levers available to our supplier client. The stores' purchase decisions, and those of the end customers they served, were driven by price.

A successful supplier must understand the competitive environ-ment faced by the direct customer and must be able to translate that understanding into concrete actions. To successfully serve the customer chain segments in this particular quadrant, the supplier's value levers must be centered on cost reduction.

This does not mean that the customers in these segments are bad customers. To the contrary, for suppliers that are well positioned to offer low prices and still realize an attractive margin, these customers are perfectly matched to their core competencies. Furthermore, the supplier can use a variety of value levers to lower prices for customers while maintaining, and even improving, margins. Engineering initiatives can create a lower-cost design. Logistics initiatives can lower the supplier's delivery costs. Lean manufacturing initiatives and purchasing initiatives can lower the cost of subcomponents and parts for the supplier.

Other value levers that yield improved margins for suppliers in this business environment involve collaborating with the direct customer: Decisions about streamlining the product or eliminating marginal services and features can yield cost savings. Efforts to integrate common activities can reduce the costs of interfacing by condensing stages of packing and unpacking. Schedule coordination and inventory sequencing can reduce downtime and help manage inventories. In our experience, many direct customers are more than willing to help the supplier uncover creative approaches to their shared problem—as long as the end result is lowered prices. Frequently, the direct customer even has a powerful sense of where savings are possible. In other cases, direct customers may be willing to make a joint investment in order to uncover potential savings. One collaborative effort involving our client uncovered areas of redundant spending (both supplier and customer were conducting quality assurance programs).

Whether the supplier chooses value levers that involve collaborative problem solving or one-sided cost reduction, the actions it takes can capture value for itself as well as its customer. If the customer chain demands these cost reductions, the supplier that can respond with creative value levers to achieve them will bring that value solution to the market segment. This will allow the supplier to capture value by sustaining or growing its volume with the customer and/or by improving its own margins on sales to these customers.

OPPORTUNITIES FOR ADDED VALUE: SYSTEMS INTEGRATION AND SERVICES

We heard very different messages from other customer chains served by this packaging supplier—in particular, the foodservice distributors who served the restaurant industry. Figure 7.5 provides some insights on how these foodservice distributors and their restaurant customers viewed their business environment:

Figure 7.5: Restaurant Takeout Packaging Customer Chain: Market Perceptions

Most of these organizations focused mainly on the tough business environment in which they operated. But the foodservice distributors understood that their own operational skills were vital. They knew that their ability to generate profits came from their own efficiency and productivity more than from any price increases they might have charged their restaurant customers.

This perspective was reiterated when we queried these organizations about how a supplier could help them be more successful. Both the foodservice distributors and the restaurants themselves emphasized opportunities within the realm of productivity and efficiency.

Figure 7.6: Restaurant Takeout Packaging Customer Chain: Needs

Supplier	Distributor	Restaurants and Fast-Food Franchises
	Needs: •"We spend a lot of time cross-docking, linking what comes in from our supplier to what goes out to our customers. If our packaging suppliers could simplify that, it would be great." •"One of our problems is multiple SKUs. Suppliers need to develop products that serve more needs"	**Needs:** •"Ways we can cut our costs are gold. We want to have our distributors bring us ideas to cut costs and improve our margins." •"Fast response— never let us run out of a key product." •"Products that simplify our operations make us faster."

These market segments fall into the lower right quadrant of the Market Map, where end customers continue to be mainly price-sensitive. The direct customer—in this case, the foodservice distributor—must once again focus on competing for the end customer's purchase on the basis of price. But when these foodservice distributors think about their relationships with suppliers, they see that their purchase decisions are based not only on price, but also on contributions that increase their efficiency and improve the margins they earn on sales to end customers. This may be a result of the fact that no one supplier is a significant part of the distributors' cost equation. For whatever reason, this customer chain, unlike our client's other market segments in the upper right quadrant, demonstrated at least a partial focus on factors other than price, as seen in figure 7.7.

Figure 7.7: Restaurant Takeout Packaging Market Map

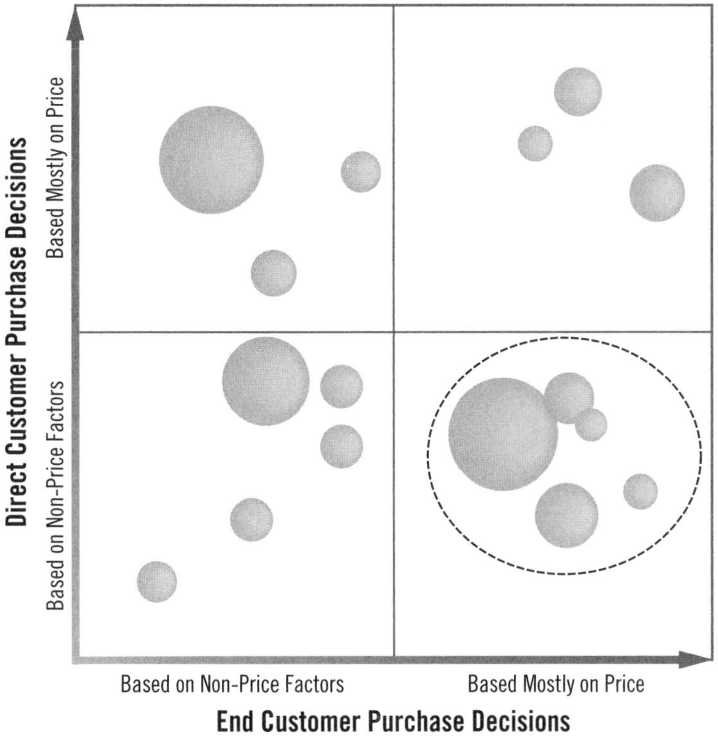

A number of value levers were available to the packaging supplier in its efforts to create value for these foodservice distributors. Several were explicitly cited by the distributors—all clustered around services and competencies that allowed them to improve productivity and efficiency. Our client chose a value lever that, in collaboration with the distributor, resulted in an improved forecasting system. The new system not only offered the supplier better visibility on future orders, but also created opportunities to appropriately bundle its products at a slight price premium for its end customers, the smaller local restaurants that wanted easy-to-use packaging materials. This value lever helped the direct customer—the distributors avoided out-of-stock items—while also streamlining the supplier's inventory carry. The supplier created value by increasing the distributors' and the restaurants' efficiency, and captured value by decreasing its own inventory costs and increasing prices on certain products.

Frequently, in business environments like the one illustrated above, the supplier can identify ways to create value levers for its direct customer by locating opportunities for all participants along the customer chain. For example, a supplier may have achieved best-in-class capabilities or economies of scale and therefore may offer the direct customer its ability to implicitly outsource those activities. This happens when the supplier is able to spread the costs of these systems and processes over a broader business base. Investment banks and law firms, for instance, take on responsibilities for their direct customers as those customers enter new global markets; the necessary expertise on financial and legal matters in each country's market would otherwise be very expensive for each individual customer to gather. Other suppliers that serve customers in global markets often find this same situation and seize the opportunity.

The potential for contributing through business services also can exist with respect to existing systems and processes that are essential to the supplier's business. When best-in-class capabilities emerge, the supplier may be able to build upon these competencies to meet the needs of its direct customer. Utilities may offer customers energy efficiency audits. Human resource consultants offer their customers courses on employment law. Environmental companies help their customers implement pollution prevention programs. All these examples reflect services that emerge from whatever core knowledge base is relevant to the supplier's business, and all of them represent services that can create value for the customer. The supplier can choose to capture this value either by charging a fee for these services or by reaching an understanding with the customer that it will be awarded more business in return for services and support.

When systems and integration services are a factor, any business customer will have a natural suspicion—after all, these propositions begin with higher costs to the supplier and somehow evolve later into total cost reductions. Relationships that are deemed strategic by both the supplier and the customer are the most likely to overcome initial suspicions. In chapter 8, we'll discuss ways for suppliers to create higher-level relationships with their business customers—an important step toward improving a firm's prospects when it offers such high-value contributions.

It is also important to note that a customer's receptivity to ideas about business systems integration and services depends heavily on how critical such systems are to the customer's core operations. If they are critical—especially if they are critical across products and/or markets—there will be great reluctance on the customer's behalf to embrace an approach that involves even implicit outsourcing. The customer that does so is making a very strong and positive statement about its supplier.

On the other hand, if the systems and processes are less critical—or if they are unique to a particular product or within a particular market—the customer is far more likely to respond favorably. In fact, the customer may applaud an idea that eliminates the need to build and manage new systems and processes. Knowing which systems and processes fall within which category can help the supplier focus its efforts in areas where success is most likely. There are numerous examples of business systems and services that have been developed and offered by innovative suppliers in recent years, such as account record-keeping services provided by American Express Travel, disposal and recycling services provided by International Paper, and training services provided by Packard Bell to its sales channel technicians.

Along with these systems and services opportunities, other value levers sometimes contribute to a business's success with customer chain segments in the lower right quadrant. While these segments are price sensitive to a degree, there are always other factors (perhaps product features or surrounding services) that also matter to the end customers. If the supplier can improve performance on one of these other factors without imposing higher costs, doing so would represent a valuable contribution to the direct customer. The reality of a tiebreaker situation ("better, cheaper, faster—pick any two") makes this task a tricky one, but one that nonetheless has been accomplished, especially when the supplier has identified new technologies and breakout concepts.

OPPORTUNITIES FOR ADDED VALUE: PRODUCT ENHANCEMENTS AND SURROUNDING SERVICES

The packaging supplier with whom we worked also served a diverse spectrum of multibillion-dollar corporations that owned a variety of branded chain restaurants and supported all the corporate business functions to be expected in Fortune 500 organizations. Our client's customer chains, therefore, included central purchasing units as well as units handling the management of restaurant operations at both corporate levels and individual sites. As we noted in chapter 2, some customer chains involve multiple organizational units within the same corporation, not all of which are "on the same page" in terms of perceptions and priorities. That was the case for many of these large chain-restaurant organizations.

Figure 7.8 provides some insights as to how the business environment was perceived by the purchasing organizations and the restaurant operations groups within these large chains.

Figure 7.8: Corporate Restaurant Customer Chain: Market Perceptions

Supplier	→	Restaurant Chain, Central Purchasing	→	Restaurant Chain, Restaurant Operations
		Market Perceptions: • "Operations must get costs down." • "Drive down the road—you'll see competitor after competitor. We have to be the best at sourcing a product at a low price." • "To make money, save money."		**Market Perceptions:** • "Our customers are looking for a positive, pleasant experience." • "Good food when they come in tonight, and tomorrow when they eat again." • "They expect convenience, from when we take the order to when they wrap the food for take-home."

Naturally, most of us hope for alignment within the organizations we serve, but our experience suggests that far too often that is not the case. In this situation, we heard divergent, confusing messages: The purchasing organizations felt that gaining lower prices from suppliers was the only route to increased profitability, while restaurant operations units were focused on the customer's dining experience. Our client wanted to understand and sort through these conflicting messages. In figure 7.9, these perceptions are translated into messages about how a supplier can create value for these restaurant chains.

Figure 7.9: Corporate Restaurant Customer Chain: Needs

Supplier	Restaurant Chain, Central Purchasing	Restaurant Chain, Restaurant Operations
	Needs: • "We expect suppliers to respond to our specs and come in with low, low prices." • "We'll disqualify a supplier that can't deliver, but the selection is based on whoever comes in with the lowest bid." • "Price, price, price."	**Needs:** • "What brings in customers and lets them leave happy is what matters to us—ideas that help are what we're looking for." • "New products that help us with the takeout business . . ." • "Appearance for the consumer is key."

The "messages from the market" provided by the executives from these restaurant chains could not have been more poorly aligned. What we heard from the purchasing organizations was one-dimensional: "Bring us lower prices." What we heard from the restaurant operations executives was focused on contributions that would yield differentiation, diner satisfaction, and innovation. In this environment, it is no wonder that our client felt schizophrenic. This is not an uncommon reaction for a supplier facing the market segments in the upper left quadrant of the Market Map (figure 7.10).

We can presume from their position on this map that the end customers (restaurant operations) would respond more positively

Figure 7.10: Corporate Restaurant Chains Market Map

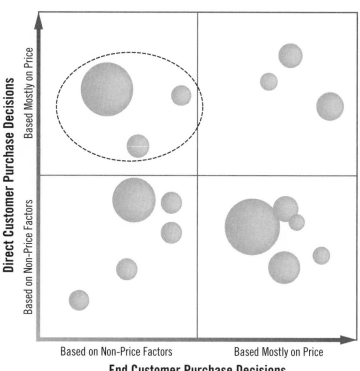

to value levers than would the direct customers (purchasing). The messages of the former, cited above, provided the packaging supplier with a clear indication of how it could focus its attention on creating value for end customers. Restaurant operators were offered and accepted a newly designed takeout container at market-based prices that provided the consumer with better use of packaging space and improved aesthetics. Takeout orders increased, creating revenue-enhanced value for the restaurants; concurrently, the supplier captured value as a consequence of increased sales with its new product line extension—which was later introduced into a different customer chain with similar success.

This example of misalignment across the departments of a large business organization mirrors the other instances illustrated in this book (particularly in chapter 6) of segments that fall within this category. In the customer chain segments in the upper left quadrant, end customers largely base their valuation on factors other than price. That is, certain product features and/or surrounding services are important to these end customers. In this same quadrant, however, the direct customers consider price a significant factor in their purchase decisions. While the restaurant's central purchasing group failed to gain a price concession from the supplier, the supplier did offer these new improvements initially at the same market-based price; as sales increased, a volume discount was factored into the contract.

Any proposed value lever must face one major hurdle before the supplier takes action: Is there explicit, price-centered proof that the added value is worth the cost? The greatest levels of frustration with the customer chains in business-to-business markets are centered in this quadrant. Suppliers experience inconsistency in how they must respond to their two customer groups, and often they find that they are unable to satisfy both consistently.

As is the case with the genuinely price-sensitive customer chain segments in the upper right quadrant of the Market Map, responding to the end customers that are sensitive to "other factors" is essential. Knowing what matters to the end customer defines what matters to the eventual business success of the direct customer, and therefore defines what matters within the supplier's management plan vis-à-vis its direct customer. The better the insights about end customers' needs and values, the better the supplier will be able to develop winning value levers—and start on the path to value capture for its shareholders.

In both this quadrant and the price-sensitive upper right quadrant, understanding the end customer is important, and this serves as the fundamental basis for strategy. In the price-sensitive quadrant, that may be enough to allow the supplier to succeed, since the direct customer's price-sensitive purchase criteria are aligned with the end customer's focus on price. In this upper left quadrant, however, where end customers' focus has shifted to product features and surrounding services, the supplier that responds to these signals may fail because of a direct customer who is oriented toward price alone. Thus the supplier is forced to invest in understanding both groups of customers and must find a way to battle through the inconsistent purchase criteria to find growth solutions.

The supplier must develop a clear understanding of the prevailing buyer behavior as well as how this may evolve. This is particularly important for business-to-business customers, given the lead times required to implement responses throughout the customer chain. Often, changes in buying behavior of the end consumer markets create problems in the supplier's relationship with its direct customer. At times, the supplier's strategy must involve partnering with the end customer to affect the purchase decisions of the direct customer. Our example in chapter 6 of a supplier to commercial vehicle manufacturers is a good example in this regard.

Failing to keep pace with changes in purchase decisions can become a major problem. If the end customers have evolved to become more price sensitive (for example, as a technology matures), the supplier that was a good partner may become a burden if it is unable to respond to a newly competitive environment. Suppliers serving direct customers in the technology industries face this problem constantly. New products are purchased on the basis of technological leadership, but they quickly evolve toward the point where price matters.

Successful suppliers in these industries are those that can evolve their offerings to match the short life cycles of their direct customers' products. At first, they must contribute through innovation and technological advancement. Soon after, they must contribute cost competitiveness while at the same time capturing value through greater volume; at this stage, familiarity and high-frequency interaction with the direct customer about the future outlook are critical. At a minimum, such steps can keep the supplier moving in the same direction as its direct customer. Yet the supplier often can go further, particularly when its own areas of expertise allow it to develop and share forecasts about how the business and technological environment might change and what will be required for both direct customer and supplier to succeed in subsequent periods.

For some suppliers, the upper left quadrant is no different from the upper right quadrant. This situation exists when the supplier's product is merely a commodity—when its products and services are truly invisible to the end customer because they are embedded in the direct customer's product. Manufacturers of many chemicals used in personal care products are an example of an "invisible" supplier. In this type of situation, the direct customer is more likely to see the supplier's significant costs as the most important dimension of the relationship, and to return discussions to that topic time and time again.

As far as the direct customer strategies go, the points discussed for the customer chain segments that fall into the upper right quadrant are relevant once again. It is important for the supplier to build an understanding of the prospective changes in purchase decisions. It can redefine its relationship with the direct customer if any such changes offer the supplier an opportunity to introduce a new value lever—one that will allow the supplier to capture value by increasing demand for products that involve the supplier's offering. Sometimes, the supplier can build a rapport with the end customer, allowing it to redefine its position: no longer an invisible commodity supplier, but an important factor in the end customer's purchase decision. For example, programs such as Energy Star (implemented by the Environmental Protection Agency and the Department of Energy) have spotlighted energy efficiency and pollution prevention in order to induce end customers to favor products that incorporate a particular supplier's products. Many suppliers have even conducted brand campaigns in order to create end customer pull-through for products that include their input. The "Intel Inside" campaign promising faster computer processing successfully created preferences for what had been a commodity input in early personal computers.

AN INVITING INVESTMENT ENVIRONMENT

The final cluster of market segments encountered by this packaging supplier is best illustrated by our discussions with executives in a number of large, family restaurant chains. These organizations were similar to the corporate restaurants described earlier, but these chains did not have dominant purchasing organizations. Rather, the key business functions in these companies were product development and restaurant operations.

The product development and restaurant operations groups were closely aligned in these organizations. Conceptually, this alignment was similar to that of the customer chain participants in the upper right quadrant, but with quite a different perspective. Instead of price, it centered on differentiated products, innovation, and breakout initiatives.

Figure 7.11 illustrates how the key participants in these customer chains viewed their market environment.

Not surprisingly, when we discussed with these business leaders how a supplier might be able to help them succeed, we heard clear messages that focused on innovation, high-value services, and contributions to brand differentiation.

Figure 7.11: Family Restaurant Customer Chain: Market Perceptions

Supplier	Family Restaurant Chain, Product Development	Family Restaurant Chain, Restaurant Operations
	Market Perceptions: • "Half of our sales is from new menu items." • "We know when we have a hit, it will be in all the competitors, so we always have to stay a step ahead of them." • "It's not just product concepts; it's how we implement them, efficiently and to please the customer."	**Market Perceptions:** • "If we're going to have customers come back week after week, we have to give them something new and interesting." • "We make the most of our money on the top end of our menu." • "If the takeout order doesn't get home fresh, that's horrible."

The contrast between the messages in this environment and those in the previous three environments presented earlier is startling. The family restaurant segments clearly belonged in the lower left quadrant of the Market Map (figure 7.13).

The suggestions about possible value levers were well aligned

Figure 7.12: Family Restaurant Customer Chain: Needs

Supplier	Family Restaurant Chain, Product Development	Family Restaurant Chain, Restaurant Operations
	Needs: • "We are very conscious of how a new product is used in the restaurant, not just how it might taste." • "Every new product presents a challenge in terms of serving it or packaging it for take-home orders." • "Can we get it to the table on time?"	**Needs:** • "The little extras are what make a difference, whether it's in the restaurant or for takeout." • "Keeping everything safe, clean, fresh-looking, inviting is key." • "You want the customer to look at the leftovers the next day and want more."

Figure 7.13: Market Map: Family Restaurant

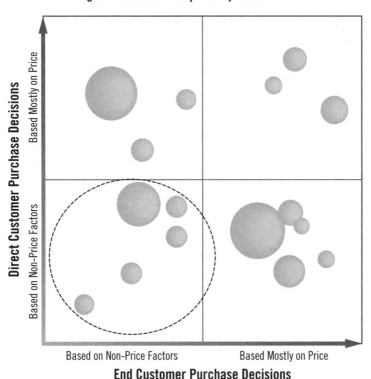

Direct Customer Purchase Decisions

Based Mostly on Price

Based on Non-Price Factors

Based on Non-Price Factors   Based Mostly on Price

End Customer Purchase Decisions

between the direct customer and the end customer; both identified contributions that would help them grow their business through product development, innovation, and differentiation. The packaging supplier learned of some interesting value lever opportunities. Its first step was to redesign the takeout packaging to ensure that the food was displayed well. When the restaurants adopted these new containers, consumers began to order desserts to take home for later. This simple switch created value for the business customer by increasing food sales and captured value for the supplier with product extension sales.

The signals coming from this environment could not be more dissimilar from those prevalent in the upper right (price-focused) quadrant that we first discussed, where our client was told to find ways to lower its prices and help its customers be more competitive. Here, the focus was on helping the business customer differentiate its products and bring new ideas and innovations to the market.

Customer chain segments that fall into the lower left quadrant are the most inviting in terms of long-term and collaborative investment opportunities. In this quadrant, the direct customer serves end customers that buy products mainly because of newer, better features and guaranteed services, not low prices. The direct customer, too, bases its purchase decisions on factors other than price. Often, this is because the supplier's costs do not significantly affect the cost structure or profit equation of the direct customer's overall product. At other times, the direct customer may have decided to seek a partnership with its supplier, and the greater focus is on meeting their mutual end customer's needs. Their combined purchase criteria create an opportunity for the supplier to create value levers. What's more, this shared motivation offers a chance for the supplier to define its investments and respond with programs that address customer needs, without creating short-term economic pressure. To the extent that the supplier can bring appealing value lever ideas to its direct customer—always with its end customer also in mind—its prospects in this environment are favorable.

The lower left quadrant presents opportunities to employ all manner of value levers as described throughout this chapter. Product features and services for the end customer, as discussed in the context of the upper left quadrant, are relevant here. Business systems integration and services provided to the direct customer, as discussed in the context of the lower right quadrant, also come into play. Businesses that have developed unique competencies or that deliver specialized services are especially likely to flourish with customer chain segments that belong to this quadrant. Ideas related to innovation, services, and other ways for suppliers to create and capture value will be further explored in later chapters. The greatest receptivity to such initiatives often occurs with customer chain segments in this quadrant.

Nevertheless, the wealth of opportunities for success in this quadrant does not guarantee the outcome. A supplier will always face challenges in spotting ways to make the direct customer's products more attractive to the end customer or to improve business systems and services. We've worked with a number of suppliers that succeeded in this environment by jointly sponsoring research with their direct customers, seeking to understand the motives of end customers in this quadrant. They've consistently reported that these collaborative investments bring great rewards, leading to innovations that serve end customer needs and to stronger foundations for the relationship between the supplier and direct customer organizations.

The nature of the business environment that exists in the lower left quadrant often makes it a spawning ground for constructive customer relationships. For the customer chain segments that dwell here, the natural discussion is about the end customer's needs, not the supplier's. Suppliers embarking on a customer management strategy alone are well advised to look for an entry within this quadrant, then evolve the relationship through thornier challenges in the other three quadrants. The next chapter explores how suppliers can create an advantage with their direct customers—typically starting with market segments in this lower left quadrant of the Market Map.

Chapter 8

INVEST IN THE RELATIONSHIP ADVANTAGE

We've seen how business customers measure value by increased market share, higher prices, or reduced costs. Product enhancements and service innovations can become powerful levers in the hands of suppliers, allowing them to create this value for their customers. When value levers help a company shift the purchase decision toward itself and away from its competitors, how can it parlay this advantage to capture greater value? Next, we'll explore how stronger relationships between suppliers and customers—co-destiny relationships—enable both organizations to grow profitably and achieve a competitive advantage in their markets.

We've worked with firms that had just secured new business and needed a strategy to ensure that the relationship was not a transient one. We've worked with companies to turn around a deteriorating relationship. And we've heard relationship horror stories from both suppliers and business customers. What we've learned is that some relationships are productive for both parties—and some simply are not meant to be. But how do you know if a more intimate relationship with a certain customer is right for your company? Once again, the answers can be found by studying the factors that drive purchase decisions along the customer chain. The customer's buying behavior typically determines whether a supplier should try to develop a "Relationship Advantage." Furthermore, when the supplier understands its customers' motivations, it can prioritize the portfolio of relationships and invest only in those that could produce a Relationship Advantage.

THE RELATIONSHIP ADVANTAGE AS A MULTIPLIER

As we consider the role of relationships in creating and capturing value, it is important to understand that the Relationship Advantage is a *multiplier,* not a stand-alone option. In business markets, we have never seen a firm that was successful only because of a Relationship Advantage. There are too many factors at work (eager competitors and sharp-penciled procurement managers come to mind) that will displace a firm—regardless of how strong the relationship may be—if it cannot meet the market in terms of price points and product and service contributions.

As we'll discuss later, investments in relationships pay dividends in markets where price competition is intense and winners are determined by low prices. While a firm operating in such an environment cannot ignore operational excellence—it must still deliver competitive prices—by investing in relationships, it can achieve a share premium vis-à-vis its competition. In many markets defined by price-based competition, this share premium can be the boost a firm needs in order to reach attractive levels of profitability. But the Relationship Advantage alternative is strong and valuable only when it complements other elements of a firm's offering.

THE RELATIONSHIP ADVANTAGE AS A PREREQUISITE

We have learned that, the Relationship Advantage frequently is a *prerequisite* for success with innovation or changes in the roles and boundaries of suppliers and their customers. We've observed far too many situations in which suppliers were thwarted in their attempts to gain new customers with a breakout offer. Their failure often was not because the technology was inadequate, but because customers lacked the solid foundation on which to balance the risks and rewards. Our research suggests that receptivity to innovation is rare unless the relationship foundation is in place. The supplier must first establish a level of confidence in its ability to execute successfully for the customer.[8]

The Relationship Advantage exists only in the context of a specific supplier-customer relationship, not an entire market or line of business. A supplier may see success in a specific relationship that has been targeted and grown through various value levers and collaborative initiatives. But when the supplier attempts to clone and transport the same practices to seemingly comparable customers, the results are typically disappointing. This is not to suggest that successful relationships are the exception, but rather that each such successful relationship is likely to be unique.

In fact, working with industry-leading firms across most business-to-business markets, we've rarely seen instances in which a supplier enjoys a Relationship Advantage with more than 40 percent of its major customers. When we include all customers—large or small, strategic or transactional—in that metric, the percentage drops dramatically.

---

8. Atlee Valentine Pope and George F. Brown, Jr., "Innovation: Fuel for Breakout Growth," *Velocity* (Fourth Quarter 2003).

BARRIERS TO BUILDING THE RELATIONSHIP ADVANTAGE

There are several reasons we don't see the Relationship Advantage more frequently. First, some customers are just unwilling to enter into an exclusive relationship with a supplier. This complex relationship is of such strategic importance to a firm's financial health that it requires unique attention, special services, and a differential status. Some customers decline to follow this approach for good business reasons, and others for reasons that may or may not be to their own advantage. Firms adopt a variety of "anti-relationship" stances, ranging from aggressive practices in supply chain management to cultivation of multiple sources to narrow boundaries that suppliers are forbidden to cross.

Second, some companies—their policies, processes, practices, people, or all of the above—simply are not compatible with strategic relationships. They may not be openly against such relationships, and they may even claim to welcome them as part of the company's vision. But the barriers that they have in place ensure that this vision is never realized.

Third, industry dynamics may limit the number of relationships a supplier can enjoy at any point in time—for example, when the relationship is defined in part by early access to new technology. Building an exclusive relationship may rule out other relationships in that same industry.

These and other issues can limit the supplier's ability to build a Relationship Advantage with certain business customers. Therefore, the supplier should follow a deliberate process in order to separate the wheat from the chaff. It must first evaluate the potential gains from a higher-level relationship with a customer organization, orienting tests toward understanding how a strategic relationship can augment the value levers it has planned for that customer. It must also scrupulously test the customer's receptivity to such a relationship. These evaluations, rather than the size of the customer or the volume of business, should provide the basis for any decision to move forward. Only when both the gains and the probability of success are above appropriate thresholds should the supplier implement programs or assign teams to build a strategic relationship with a customer.

We've conducted substantial research to help our clients learn how to build a Relationship Advantage. In the 1990s, we performed in-depth interviews with suppliers and their customers to understand what defined relationships of different levels. During 2001 and 2002, we collaborated with the Strategic Account Management Association on a research project to understand the links between strategic account relationships and growth.[9] In 2003, with a focus on the automotive industry, we examined the pricing pressures that often accompany supplier-customer relationships and the actions that both participants were using to achieve positive outcomes.[10] In 2005, we studied the ways in which suppliers could become solutions providers in support of their key customers.[11]

This research has confirmed our conclusion: Specific behaviors contribute to success in strategic business-to-business relationships.

---

9. See www.strategicaccounts.org for information on this organization. For a description of this research project, see Atlee Valentine Pope and George F. Brown, Jr., "Whatever Happened to Growth?" *Velocity* (Fourth Quarter 2001). Several other papers published in *Velocity* summarize key insights developed as a result of this research project.
10. See Atlee Valentine Pope, Jon T. Gabrielsen, and George F. Brown, Jr., *Win the Day: Managing Price Pressures in the Automotive Industry* (Chicago: Blue Canyon Partners, Inc., 2003).
11. See Atlee Valentine Pope, E. Shawn O'Donnell, and George F. Brown, Jr., *Translating Solutions into Rewards for Customers and Shareholders* (Evanston, IL: Blue Canyon Partners, Inc., 2006).

Certain key metrics important to the firms involved—profitability, growth, stability, receptivity to innovation, and evolution of the relationship into new settings—can measure this success. It should come as no surprise that the strongest relationships are those that manage to facilitate and augment the three approaches to value creation and value capture.

THE RELATIONSHIP ADVANTAGE IN THE
LOWER LEFT QUADRANT

The Relationship Advantage can help companies create and capture value in each of the four market segments identified in the Market Map. First among these is the situation that exists in the lower left quadrant of the map, where both direct customers and end customers are focused primarily on non-price factors (such as product attributes, technology, or enhanced services) in their purchase decisions. The supplier's greatest threat in this environment is a competitor's offer that fulfills the customer's highest-priority needs for improved product, services, or technology. Therefore, to anticipate and ward off potential threats, the supplier in this environment should focus first and foremost on its own investments. It must create a game plan that ensures it will be first to market with the superior product and service.

In this lower-left-quadrant environment, it is less likely that a competitor who offers a lower-priced, unenhanced product will win out over an incumbent supplier with a superior product and service offer. No incumbent supplier can ever totally ignore price competition, but its response should focus on the non-price factors critical to the customer—not mimic the competition by focusing on price.

When we interview business customers in this market environment, remarkably often they tell us that they run price-based competitions because "all the suppliers are the same. None of them bring anything new or better to the table." Yet these customers are quick to list their own wish lists of improvements in the products and services that they hope to receive from one of those competitors.

The Relationship Advantage significantly multiplies the supplier's efforts to focus on delivering a product and service advantage rather than competing on price. There are two reasons for this. First, with the Relationship Advantage, the client can build the foundation necessary for successful innovation. Earlier, we noted the reluctance of most customers to embrace an innovation unless the appropriate relationship with the supplier is in place. Our research is very convincing: The firm with the Relationship Advantage is the only firm that will enjoy the benefit of such a foundation. The second reason is that firms with a Relationship Advantage are far more likely than others to collaborate with their customers on new products and new technologies. With the customer as your partner in innovations, no competitor will find it easy to gain entry on price alone.

THE RELATIONSHIP ADVANTAGE IN THE
UPPER RIGHT QUADRANT

The Relationship Advantage is also important at the opposite end of the Market Map. In the upper-right-quadrant environment, both direct customers and end customers focus heavily on price when making their purchase decisions. The entire customer chain tends to emphasize a bare-bones offering. Customers in this environment rarely reward suppliers for offering services that are meant to enhance the prod-uct; not only that, but they also often bring competition to the table, seeking a lower bid. As a result, the biggest threat to a supplier in this environment comes from a competitor that offers lower prices for essentially the same product or service bundle.

Even for the most imaginative supplier, the alternatives to a price-based response are quite limited. It is in this market environment that we most often see vicious cycles of price-based competition. Ultimately, long-term success belongs to the firms with superior cost structures, in their own operations and in their supply bases. Lessons from this environment, however, do not travel well into the other three environ-ments, and firms that accept price-based competition as their standard mode of behavior often lose customers and margin at once.

Clearly, in this upper right quadrant the most important foothold is not the Relationship Advantage but the cost advantage. And to be successful, the supplier must use its cost advantage to either preempt its competition or respond successfully to competitive overtures based on price. Once again, however, the Relationship Advantage creates a value lever for the supplier.

In this environment, the Relationship Advantage contributes in three ways. First, and perhaps most important, the firm that achieves a higher-level relationship typically gains a "last look" at opportunities with its customers. As the incumbent, it is in a position to retain the business—as long as it can meet market pricing. This is an enormous advantage to a supplier. While it doesn't guarantee that all business will be retained, it means that the supplier has a choice: Is the busi-ness worth retaining or not? It means that the supplier can win in a tiebreaker situation, avoiding the vicious pricing cycle. For many sup-pliers, their ability to gain a share premium makes all the difference between bottom-line success and bottom-line failure, given the economics of their business and the important role of volume in covering fixed costs. The Relationship Advantage gives the supplier the maximum possible opportunity to achieve a share advantage.

The other two reasons for focusing on the Relationship Advantage in this price-sensitive environment are especially of consequence in certain settings. The firm that enjoys a Relationship Advantage typically has superior knowledge available to it in shaping its offers and bids. Because it knows what matters to the customer, it can avoid, for example, losing a key relationship in a reverse auction because it isn't getting the right information.

The final method for translating a Relationship Advantage into a major win in this market environment is admittedly both risky and rarely used, though we've seen it on occasion. Sometimes the customer's obsession with price is misguided or rests on shaky ground; there may in fact be alternative ways for the supplier to succeed in its markets. But broaching the subject is bound to be tricky—the supplier must not seem to be one-upping the customer in its own business arena. Even the supplier who recognizes this opening has a chance of successfully making its case only if it has a very strong relationship with the customer. Without the foundation of a strong Relationship Advantage, such an argument may reach the customer's door but will likely be dead on arrival.

THE RELATIONSHIP ADVANTAGE IN THE
LOWER RIGHT QUADRANT

The Relationship Advantage plays a different, much more complicated role in the complex lower right quadrant. Here, end customers focus primarily on price, while direct customers incorporate non-price factors into their purchase decisions. As we've discussed, this can happen when the supplier's product represents a very small portion of its customer's cost structure; even if the supplier raises the price of its products materially, this may essentially make no difference in the prices seen by the end customer.

This environment tends to be jumbled; the competition among suppliers is fierce, and business customers don't have a clear idea of what they're looking for. Their own customers are always pressuring them on price, but they realize that their supplier's price isn't a big part of their cost equation. This makes the supplier's cost advantage nearly irrelevant. At the same time, though, these customers aren't likely to reward a supplier's product or technology advantages, as they know that their own customers care more about price. Naturally, they would rather pay lower prices than higher prices. But all other things being equal, they'll certainly welcome the supplier's product and service advantages—at least when they can use these advantages to tout their own products—as long as there is no cost implication. Some customers will even establish scoring systems that rank these product and service advantages; a firm may try to match its own competitive strategy, which could involve both meeting market-based prices and citing its product's advantages over competitors'. Frankly, we're convinced that both these advantages—the cost advantage and the product and service advantage—are minor ones. Neither is likely to create a compelling response to a competitor's overture in this intricate business environment.

What *can* make a difference in this environment is any initiative that changes the game for the supplier-customer team. This is where firms with a Relationship Advantage can win over those that do not enjoy this advantage.

In this environment, the potential exists for game-changing contributions when the supplier can build a strong enough relationship that its direct customer allows it to bring innovative approaches to taking cost out of the supplier-customer system and create savings. When a firm can identify and act on value levers that remove costs from the supplier-customer system, it achieves the win-win goal: creating value for its customer and capturing value for its own shareholders. Not every supplier, obviously, can identify such value levers. Those that can build a strong foundation with their customer, however, will be in a position to thwart competitive efforts based on price. If there is a strong Relationship Advantage in place, the customer will be far more open and willing to work with the supplier on these cost-saving initiatives.

We worked closely with one firm that had important market segments in the lower right quadrant. Its own product accounted for less than 1 percent of the cost of the subsequent products manufactured by its direct customers. As we drew up detailed economic models of the business relationship between this firm and its customers, we discovered that an additional 12 percent of the direct customer's cost structure involved adjacency costs—costs connected closely to the product our client supplied. These ranged from labor costs associated with the manufacturing process to warranty costs linked with product failure. By developing several options and taking action, our client was able to drive significant cost savings in these adjacency categories, without dramatic increases in the cost of their own product. Some of these contributions had multiplier advantages that saved well in excess of $10 for every $1 spent.

Not all of the firm's direct customers were willing to embrace these adjacency savings. Their caution was based on uncertainty about locking into a relationship with this supplier, particularly as some of the ideas required them to make design changes. The relationship foundation that is prerequisite to success with game-changing ideas just wasn't there. The relationship had to reach a higher level for the customer to have confidence and comfort with such game-changing initiatives—a step that will be discussed in the next several chapters of this book.

With a Relationship Advantage, suppliers and customers can cooperate to develop a win-win strategy. Simply stated, the team has more to work with than when the two organizations look at their parts in isolation. We've provided many examples of suppliers who have created and captured value using initiatives that remove cost from the system, and a Relationship Advantage has played an important role in almost every one. In fact, many of these success stories are told to us by customers about their favorite suppliers. Achieving such results occurs only when there is a Relationship Advantage.

THE RELATIONSHIP ADVANTAGE IN THE
UPPER LEFT QUADRANT

The upper left quadrant involves end customers that focus on factors other than price and direct customers that emphasize price in their buying behavior—another complex environment. The supplier that offers lower price points certainly is responding to the direct customers' messages, but at the expense of its own margins. In some instances, lowering prices may be the only option available to suppliers—they can do nothing to create value for the participants along the customer chain, making it difficult for them to capture a share premium or a price premium for their direct customer.

In many other instances, however, the supplier can encourage success and growth without an adverse impact on prices and margins. To do so, it must provide superior product and service contributions that are visible and important to end customers. The commercial vehicle supplier in chapter 6, whose products were sought by the end customers, is one such example. In that instance, the supplier coupled enhanced offerings with direct outreach to the end customers, in order to build awareness and confidence in its products and support services. The key to this strategy is that the end customer must be aware of the supplier's contribution, at which point it should be willing to develop a Relationship Advantage with the supplier.

One final takeaway from this lesson about the Relationship Advantage: Success is far more likely for a firm that is proactive than for one that is reactive to competitors' actions. True, building a higher-level relationship with a direct customer may open the door for game-changing innovations, or it may help your firm develop end customer preferences as a source of pull-through demand. But this can't be achieved at the last minute. Best-practice firms recognize early on the most intriguing value levers in each environment. From the beginning, they work on value creation responses that build on the product, service, and relationship advantages.

Now that you've learned how to *create* value for your customers, it's time to learn how you can *capture* that value for your own organization. The first step is to develop a successful Go-to-Market Strategy.

SECTION II: DEVELOP YOUR GO-TO-MARKET STRATEGY

Chapter 9

DEVELOP YOUR PRODUCT AND BRAND STRATEGY

If the case studies of the previous chapters show one thing, perhaps it is this: Developing strategies to create and capture value in business markets is a sizeable task. When customer chains are complex, the supplier must consider the factors that drive the purchase decisions at each stage of the chain. Company leaders must choose the value levers that will allow firms to turn value creation into value capture. Only the firm that is successful in creating and capturing value will realize success in the marketplace; to do so, its value creation contributions must be reinforced across all the elements of its business strategy, including product and brand decisions (discussed in this chapter), services (chapter 10), and pricing (chapter 11).

We can build upon the framework we've developed to examine some of the other key decisions faced by a firm, namely, those relating to acquisitions (chapter 13) and the selection of customers across new markets, especially from among new global markets (chapter 14). What emerges from this section as a whole is an integrated portrait of

Figure 9.1: Product and Brand Placement Market Map

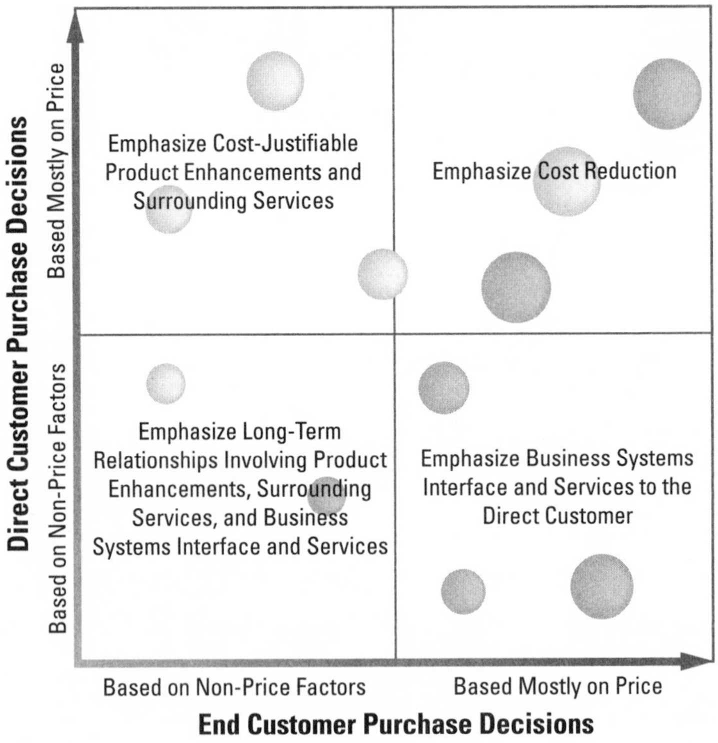

how the firm can make its key decisions in a way that is consistently oriented toward the goal of creating and capturing value.

In order to create value, it is necessary to understand what is important from the perspective of each customer along the customer chain. Figure 9.1, above, which we developed as a Market Map, provides a starting point for our discussion of product and brand decisions as part of an overall strategy for going to market.

MATCHING PRODUCT STRATEGY TO CUSTOMERS' CRITICAL SUCCESS FACTORS

In the upper-right-quadrant business environment, the direct customers and the end customers are aligned; in their purchase decisions, they focus on price. In that environment, successful product offerings are likely to be bare-bones offerings with limited enhancements, ones that just meet the customers' specs. Similarly, service offerings should be limited in scope—the minimal ones demanded by customer chain participants. The most successful channels to market are likely to be those that are highly efficient, delivering products and services at a minimum cost burden. Pricing is the basis of competitive success in this environment, and investments in innovation are likely to yield wins only if they generate an improved cost position.

The lower left quadrant is the business environment that differs most from the one described above. The customer chain is once again aligned across direct and end customers, but the alignment is based on buying behavior that considers factors other than price. Product strategy in this market segment should reflect best-in-class offerings, typically with significant features and enhancements that are upscale in the context of the market being served. Similarly, service offerings that bring value to customer chain participants—support that makes a significant contribution to value creation for these customers—are likely to be well received and rewarded. Investments in product and service innovations are generally recognized and compensated, too. Overall, channels that contribute value and are a cut above in performing their roles and responsibilities are preferred in this business environment.

While price can never be ignored, it is typically a secondary factor for firms that can differentiate their position in terms of these other elements of a Go-to-Market Strategy.

For a firm offering a product family that spans a Good-Better-Best spectrum, these two market segments frequently define the extremes. The Good offering designed for the upper right quadrant is a much more basic product, with limited features and surrounding services, sold at a lower price point. The Better product represents an intermediate offering in terms of product features, surrounding services, and

Figure 9.2: Good, Better, Best Market Map

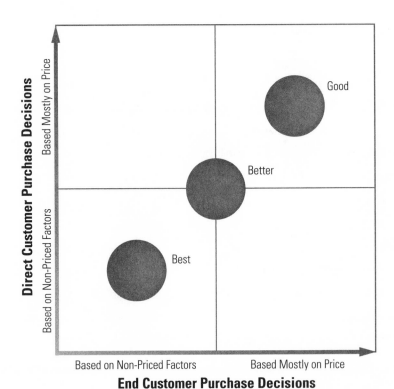

price. The Best offering, often targeted toward customers in the lower left quadrant, typically involves superior product features, surrounded by services, at a premium price. Figure 9.2 suggests this Good–Better–Best spectrum in the context of the purchase decision drivers for both the direct customer and the end customer.

In a general sense, the message that is presented to the market for the Best offering is this: It is the one that the customer would select if price were not a consideration. Offerings at this end of the product spectrum also communicate the product's exceptional features and the technical competencies of the supplier. Typically, the supplier selects the Best product offering to be linked closely to its corporate brand. In circumstances where the supplier is able to anchor its major customer relationships through segments in the lower left quadrant, even greater importance is attached to the brand messages associated with the Best offering.

We worked with one client organization that built complex cooling towers and other heat transfer products for use by industrial facilities and in power plants. Even in this complex, technical arena, where each site required a specific and customized solution, the organization's offerings spanned a Good–Better–Best spectrum. The products at the Good end of the spectrum still incorporated significant technology and addressed the heat management needs of customers. But at the Best end of the spectrum, our client's offerings incorporated more and more technology. Some of this technology was linked to singular challenges at certain customer sites—water scarcity, operations near urban environments, limited site footprint, highly complex operations (such as nuclear power plants). Not all customers needed the technologies incorporated into these Best products, and to meet their diverse needs, our client's offerings spanned a spectrum of capabilities. But to a significant extent, the firm's reputation was based on its ability to solve the challenges using its Best products.

Often the midrange Better product offering reflects a subset of the capabilities incorporated into the Best offering and is frequently presented as a sub-brand, perhaps endorsed by the supplier's primary corporate brand. Using this practice, the supplier can link its product and service competencies with the Better product while still putting out a price-product-service combination that is appropriate for its target intermediate market.

Suppliers make brand decisions about the Good product offering with various motivations in mind. In some cases, the distance between the Best and Good offerings is so great that no brand linkages are made. This type of Good offering may actually be presented through a private label used by sales channel partners or in separate, unconnected brands, defined by a message of affordability. In other instances, the Good offerings may remain in the fold—providing they're similar enough to the product and service of the corporate brand to warrant sub-brand treatment.

Products evolve (or devolve) along the Good-Better-Best spectrum over time; we are all aware of products that were Best yesterday but only Good today. Many firms—especially those in such industries as telecommunications, pharmaceuticals, computers, and others involving fast-changing technology—take up the primary challenge of developing and transitioning their products according to plans that constantly refresh the offering at the Best end of the spectrum. It is essential to learn from their customers which features will be critical to the Best products of tomorrow. A company must count on this type of forward thinking to sustain success in business environments where purchase decisions are driven by factors other than price.[12]

In the other two quadrants of the Market Map, the customer chain is not aligned. In the lower right quadrant, end customers are focused on price, but direct customers emphasize other factors in their purchase decisions. The supplier must decide on the preferred mix of strategy elements, as participants reflect characteristics of both the price-focused and the quality-focused environments. Product offerings are typically bare-bones and, once again, just meet the specs; any enhancements are limited to those that enable the direct customer to otherwise save money (for example, by streamlining its own manufacturing process). Important success stories from suppliers operating in these markets reveal careful observation of how customers use their products; the clever supplier then reengineers the products to streamline the customer's processes. The result is a value contribution that enables its customers to save money. Firms that respond effectively to the challenges of this business environment are more likely to capture value by gaining a share premium rather than a price premium.

In the upper left quadrant, the direct customers are focused on price (perhaps because their philosophy values aggressive supply chain management) even though their end customers emphasize other factors in their purchase decisions. Product features and service enhancements can be successful in this environment, but only if they are visible to and perceived as valuable by end customers. Success stories often involve important ingredients, where the supplier can establish a strong preference among its end customers; as mentioned

---

12. See Jon T. Gabrielsen and Bruce B. Karr, *Customer-Driven Product Development* (Evanston, IL: Blue Canyon Partners, Inc., 2006).

earlier, the "Intel Inside" campaign represents the textbook definition of successful ingredient positioning. Suppliers in any number of
business markets have been similarly successful in gaining customer
support from later stages along the customer chain; these participants
then demand that the ingredients be included in the products they
buy. This market environment is often one of supplier-customer or
supplier-channel conflict and competition for margin. As a result,
pricing is likely to be driven to market levels, and the supplier's best
hopes of capturing value will involve share premiums and a lowered
cost of sales and service, rather than price premiums.

DEVELOPING THE PRODUCT SPECTRUM

Many business markets involve end customers that are likely to migrate
along the Good–Better–Best product spectrum over time, for example, as product technology evolves or as a function of their purchasing
power. Successful brand architecture can play a crucial role: It builds
global loyalty that can tie the end customer to both the supplier and
the direct customer or sales channel partner. Brand messages can con-
vey product features and services that are consistent across the Good–
Better–Best range—or that at least provide familiar options along this
spectrum. Assessing the degree of separation of alternative customer
chain segments is thus a critical fact to consider in defining brand
architectures for Good–Better–Best product spectrums. If segments are
not too distant, it typically makes sense to connect them in the brand
architecture. If they are far apart in terms of the factors that drive purchase decisions, connections may cause confusion.

Marriott International is an excellent example of a company that built a brand architecture for its Good-Better-Best products, which are located across several quadrants in the Market Map illustrated below (figure 9.3). By the early 1980s, Marriott had become the single largest operator of hotel rooms in the United States. As Marriott expanded its hospitality offerings, it focused on further developing its Best and Better categories. Over time, Marriott developed a significant portfolio of lodging brands. Most of these are targeted at businesses, including both direct customers (the corporate travel department) and

Figure 9.3: Marriott Brands Market Map

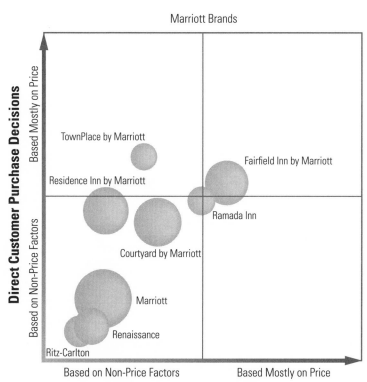

End Customer Purchase Decisions

end customers (the individual traveler), as well as other market segments such as vacationers.

Brands in the Best category (in the lower left quadrant) include the Ritz-Carlton brand, a worldwide symbol of prestige and distinction in luxury lodging, and the Renaissance Hotels and Resorts. Even more prominent within this Best category are the Marriott Hotels, Resorts and Suites, the company's flagship corporate brand. These brands target the upscale business traveler and corporate meeting planners—end customers who can take advantage of full-service accommodations, including business centers, meeting facilities, and conference and banquet facilities. For many years, Marriott built its quality name and reputation by designing, building, and managing its own hotels. Today, the Marriott brand is well recognized as a symbol of consistently high quality and dependable, friendly service.

During the 1980s, Marriott recognized the opportunity to develop new hotel chains for business travelers looking for different products, reflected in new price points and also in available services and the rooms themselves. Marriott began by addressing the needs of the business traveler who stayed at mid-level hotels or motels; it focused on establishing a Better lodging offering as a sub-brand chain. Its research on the buying preferences of these business travelers indicated that room quality and outdoor surroundings mattered most to this target market. Consequently, Marriott created Courtyard by Marriott, a moderately priced lodging chain with the slogan "Courtyard by Marriott—Designed by Business Travelers for Business Travelers." Courtyard's rooms are close in quality to the full-service rooms in the Best category, and each location has a landscaped courtyard. In order to offer moderate prices, Courtyard has small meeting rooms and does not offer room service. Nevertheless, because the value-conscious business traveler knows that Courtyard is a Marriott-owned institution, the traveler implicitly perceives that the Marriott endorsement means the Courtyard rooms and service will be of a professional, consistent quality at a satisfactory, moderate price.

Further up and to the right in figure 9.3 is the Ramada Inn chain. This mid-priced hotel brand is designed differently than the Courtyard brand; still at a modest price, it offers meeting and banquet facilities to business travelers. Ramada Inn is the only brand that does not carry the explicit "by Marriott" modifier, because it is the only brand in the portfolio that is not fully managed and directly under Marriott's control. Marriott operates Ramada Inn franchises, and it licenses the use of the Ramada Inn brand name to other lodging companies in North America. Because of this arrangement, Marriott has less control over the operations of these hotels, and thus it elects not to link the Ramada Inn brand name with its corporate brand, which is associated with consistency, dependability, and friendliness.

The Fairfield Inn by Marriott rounds out the brand portfolio. This economy-priced brand appeals to business and leisure travelers who seek quality accommodations at a less expensive price point. This brand is positioned between the Better and Good categories, and it carries the Marriott corporate brand-name modifier to distinguish it from its independent chain competitors and other chains, which might not meet the standards of quality and consistency of a Marriott-brand facility. And yet this brand certainly is still far from the upper right corner of the Market Map, with messages to customers that emphasize value, not just low price.

Marriott has also built brands to attract extended-stay business travelers. Guest suites at the Residence Inn by Marriott are known for their "home away from home" image and offer many amenities, from separate living and sleeping areas to complimentary breakfast to fully equipped kitchens. The Residence Inn is a Better brand, positioned close to the TownePlace by Marriott brand. TownePlace is the company's mid-priced, extended-stay brand with very similar amenities, but to meet these prices, housekeeping services are provided on a weekly (not daily) basis. Like the Courtyard brand, Residence Inn and TownePlace are branded with the Marriott modifier so the business traveler and the corporate travel department can associate these operations with Marriott's well-known, dependable quality and service.

Marriott has instituted other mechanisms to bolster its market-oriented messages to the corporate travel department and the business traveler. Following the example of airlines, Marriott has long offered price discounts to corporations that are willing to underwrite exclusive contracts stipulating that their business travelers will stay at Marriott hotels. They also offer extensive conference and meeting services to their corporate customers. To complement these arrangements with the direct customer, Marriott has a frequent-guest bonus program that awards points to the business traveler, who can use these points to stay at any one of the Marriott-owned hotels or resorts. Marriott also operates a common computerized reservation system for all these brands, providing a productivity tool that benefits both the direct customer and the end customer. Marriott thus presents an excellent example of how a company can develop products and brands as part of a Go-to-Market Strategy developed for distinct quadrants across the Market Map.

AVOIDING A FOCUS ON ONLY ONE
BUSINESS ENVIRONMENT

Over and over, we've observed situations in which decisions about product development and investments in innovation were made as if all the targeted markets were located in the lower left quadrant of the Market Map. Countless sources of excitement and stimulation give rise to this outcome: Engineers and designers believe they can take the products "to the next level." Sales team members cite a competitor's "better offer" that they're convinced has cost them the sale. Creative managers want to apply ideas inspired by some insight from another industry. All these triggers lead to plans to enhance products, add new features and capabilities, and otherwise augment the existing offering.

But when targeting customer chains in the other three quadrants, these efforts may not be appropriate. In the upper right quadrant, new features and capabilities—and the added costs they bring—are often 180 degrees off course. Why? In this environment, as we know by now, customers are focused on price and looking for a simple, inexpensive solution that meets their needs.

We worked with a client that provided automation and control solutions to customers in the chemicals industry. This firm was a leader in terms of innovation, and it constantly was raising the bar in terms of its product quality and flexibility. To a certain extent, its product development decisions were driven by internal experts who were proud of their many patents and awards. In addition, the firm was influenced heavily by some major customers in the pharmaceuticals segment of the market—organizations that applauded each time the bar was raised.

When we developed the Market Map for this customer, we found that a significant portion of its market was located in the upper right quadrant—customers that were in commodity chemicals businesses where price pressures were intense and margins were often nonexistent. This segment of the industry provided a simple message, namely, "We need a cheaper solution." Over time, these customers' purchases evolved toward a competitor whose offer was past-generation technology, sold at a very low price point. Their unspoken message to our client was this: "While we are in awe of the technology, it makes no business sense for us, and even if it did, we couldn't afford it." For environments such as this one, the ideal strategy is oriented toward reaching lower and lower price points. Firms in this situation need to focus product development efforts on building a "standard" product that can be profitably sold at a lower price point than their existing offerings. By taking this approach, a firm can capture value from market segments where customer needs are less complex and price is a key factor in decision making.

We worked with another firm that prides itself on its capability to engineer its products to lower and lower prices. The CEO of this firm has set timetables within which product costs must be halved, and the engineering team has taken on the challenge of exceeding these goals—and it usually does. The underlying belief throughout this firm is that it has to not only deliver products at that Best end of the spectrum, but also win the large and lucrative Good market from its competitors.

Delivering the ideal product when your customer chain lies in the two other quadrants of the Market Map is a more complex process. In the upper left quadrant, raising the bar can provide an advantage, as long as the improvements are visible and important to the end custom-ers. When that is the case, the supplier's superior offering and brand are likely to create "pull" from the end customers, which can offset the direct customer's price-centered focus. Any firm that has implemented an ingredients-branding strategy to ward off price pressures from its direct customers likely operates in this upper left quadrant. Efforts at creating end customer demand for its ingredient are pivotal in such quests to avoid commoditization by the direct customer. Examples of this are prevalent across many industries—notably, the makers of such products as Fuller transmissions for trucks and Bose consumer elec-tronics for cars.

In the lower right quadrant, where end customers are focused on price, additional product features and enhanced capabilities are likely to get the same response that occurs in the upper right quadrant—customers will gladly take them, but they aren't likely to pay extra for them. Product development efforts that reduce costs are most likely to be successful in this environment. Direct customers who prefer the opportunity to implement innovations will be pleased when these adjustments reduce costs in their own operations. Recall the firm that gained significant share through a product development initiative that did nothing other than make its product easier to use by its direct customers; this is a dramatic story of a success that didn't involve new features or technology, just simplification.

We've already discussed the opportunities that exist to create a Rela-tionship Advantage, which can change the roles of and the boundaries between a firm and its business customers. Product innovations that achieve cost savings or otherwise simplify and streamline operations are far more likely to be successful when a Relationship Advantage exists.

This chapter has focused primarily on product strategy, an important element of any firm's Go-to-Market Strategy and its brand position. Other factors, such as pricing and services, are also important; in fact, as has been suggested in this chapter's examples, they're often the differentiating factors in some market environments. In the next two chapters, we'll focus more directly on how services can be managed as tools to help create and capture value—and how firms can manage the inevitable pricing pressures that will come from the actions of customers and competitors.

Chapter 10

DELIVER VALUE THROUGH SERVICES

Let's revisit the packaging supplier from chapter 7 and its numerous opportunities for value creation, looking again at the messages that involved service strategies. Our client's business customers included foodservice distributors who focused their attention on services to help them manage inventory and out-of-stock situations. The end customers in this case included restaurant executives who focused their attention on new product development and appearance, among other factors. But while this case study spotlighted value creation through services, many business leaders question the role that services should play in developing an overall Go-to-Market Strategy that creates value that will be recognized and rewarded by their customers.

THE SERVICES PARADOX

A recent event illustrates this disparity. We had the opportunity to discuss service strategies at a conference attended by executives from a wide spectrum of business-to-business suppliers. During the lunch prior to our presentation on this topic, we sat at two different tables and heard two very different views of service offerings.

At one table, an individual from the automotive parts industry said, "We all have to accept market-based pricing. Product and technology differentiation lasts about ten minutes. When it really comes down to it, we have to compete and win business on services." The other individuals seated at that table—from such industries as chemicals, glass, telecommunications, and industrial equipment—offered example after example supporting this statement. Each told of some customer whose business was won or retained on the basis of superior or unique service offerings. The conversation then shifted to the tremendous obstacle of figuring out what services a supplier could offer that would achieve the same types of successes. As one participant in the conversation pointed out, "The problem is that there are no patterns to follow."

At the other table, an office equipment company president stated, "I've always viewed services as the hole in the income statement out of which profits drain." Individuals seated at that table—representing suppliers of chemicals, electrical equipment, computers, packaging systems, and capital goods—followed his comments with their own horror stories of customers who failed to recognize the value of services or reward their firm for providing them. "We respond to all the demands for services," one business veteran observed, "and then get the rug pulled out from under us at contract time." Many at the table nodded their heads in agreement.

When we compared notes about these conversations, we were not surprised. No business-to-business supplier that we know is without a story in either direction. These business leaders understand that providing services can be the route to both success and bankruptcy—perhaps even at the same time.

Services largely remain a paradox to many business-to-business suppliers. Some key customers insist on the value of services, but purchasing organizations often give no credit to suppliers that provide them. Yet the services paradox must be resolved—especially as suppliers begin to apply emerging technologies to their business processes and to contemplate using service strategies to strengthen their value proposition.

We believe that the complex customer chains served by suppliers are at the root of the services paradox. There are many types of business-to-business customer chains. A few were showcased in earlier chapters—sequential manufacturing processes exist within the automotive industry, sales channel partner relationships prevail in the foodservice industry, franchise relationships are common in many sectors of the economy, and centralized purchasing structures support a host of end customers throughout the same organization.

In all these customer chains, the supplier faces the distinct challenge of serving multiple customers. The direct customer and the end customers may differ considerably on their valuation of any particular service. And, across the many customer chains that exist within a market, there is enormous potential for inconsistency.

THREE TYPES OF SERVICE OFFERINGS

We believe that services can be relevant to success in markets involving complex customer chains. We've identified three distinct classes of services across business markets. First, there are services aimed at the end customer; tire warranties on new cars, manufacturer financing on a new computer, and frequent flyer miles to business travelers are examples within this category. Second, there are services provided to the end customer through an active, collaborative process that involves both the supplier and the direct customer. Examples of these services include upgrades and product modernization, installation of automotive parts at service centers, installation of electrical equipment by contractors, and training provided to end customers in the use of a product. A third class includes services visible only to the supplier's direct customer and oriented solely toward creating value for that customer. Engineering contributions to product design, training for a value-added reseller's sales force, and record keeping for the corporate travel department are examples in this category.

To make appropriate service decisions as part of a successful Go-to-Market Strategy, the supplier must understand fully the factors that drive purchase decisions on the part of each participant in the customer chain. Does the direct customer make purchase decisions strictly on the basis of price, or is it willing to pay higher prices in order to obtain particular product features or services? The end customers served through the customer chain must also be evaluated as to their purchasing criteria—along a spectrum ranging from decisions driven by price to those where product and service considerations dominate.

Figure 10.1 illustrates how a supplier can make effective service decisions as part of an overall Go-to-Market Strategy. Customer segments within the upper right quadrant are unlikely to appreciate, or to be willing to pay for, most services. The message provided by one supplier's customer was clear: "Don't they get it? We want them to stop spending money on services and reduce their prices instead." The appropriate services strategy to offer these customers is the one that meets, at minimum cost, the specification defined by the customer. Returning to the comments made during the lunch table discussions, those who described services as "the hole in the income statement"

Figure 10.1: Services and Strategy Market Map

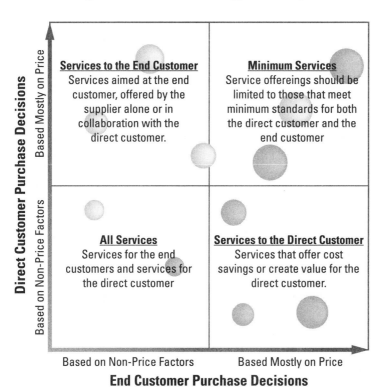

Based on Non-Price Factors   Based Mostly on Price

End Customer Purchase Decisions

most likely reflected experiences with customers in this business environment. Customers in this environment will always accept services, but they won't reward the supplier that provides them.

End customers that dwell within the lower right quadrant probably will offer much the same message. However, the supplier that concentrates service offerings on its direct customer (or sales channel partner) can create and capture value in return for these services. The emphasis placed by the foodservice distributors on productivity and efficiency is an example of where and how value can be created in this environment. In many regards, this business environment offers the most complex service challenges—and it also suggests enormous potential.

Many of the most successful business-to-business Internet-enabled service offerings—such as quote and order status, technical support with chat rooms, and cross-reference for brands and product SKUs—have been targeted at customer chain segments within this business environment. We've also seen business-to-business suppliers achieve success in their own efforts to globalize by offering globalization services to support the parallel efforts of their major customers. All these services respond to the needs for efficiency and productivity on the part of the supplier's direct customer—the basic mandate for success in the lower-right-quadrant business environment.

End customers within the upper left quadrant, unlike those in the two business environments described previously, are likely to value service offerings. The supplier often finds, however, that it must compete with the direct customer or sales channel partner to capture the value associated with such services. All too often, the direct customer attempts to manage the supplier into a position of commodity provider, and thus maintain sole ownership of the relationship. The one-dimensional emphasis of the purchasing executives in the restaurant chains is an example of barriers to value creation for end customers in this business environment. The failure of organizations to align purchasing department objectives (lower cost) with end customer priorities (more innovation) extends beyond that example, creating countless challenges for suppliers that are touched by this market segment. Another frequent cause of misalignment in this environment is profit pressures that drive direct customers to strive for gains at the expense of their suppliers. The comments about customers saying one thing but doing another at contract time almost always emerge from this business environment.

Service strategies in this environment, therefore, are most likely to succeed when they are integrated with an explicit branding program oriented toward the end customer. Sometimes this can be done in a way that connects with the direct customer's or sales channel partner's message. In many instances, though, it must be done so that the end customer is the one to place pressure on the direct customer or sales channel partner. One way or the other, successes in this environment require efforts to create preferred relationships between suppliers and their end customers.

The greatest potential for success with a broad array of service offerings exists within the lower left quadrant. Here, there is alignment throughout the customer chain, and the supplier has the potential to create and capture value by providing services to direct and end customers alike—and can even anticipate cooperation from the direct customer in creating services and delivering them to the end customer. It is within this business environment that the longest and most stable relationships exist, with services often compromising a key part of these relationships; as a result, competitors at each stage in the customer chain face significant barriers to their efforts to gain share.

A key lesson for business-to-business suppliers emerges from the consideration of these four distinct business environments: Any single services strategy will be greeted differently across market segments and customers. The only correct services decisions are those that manage to incorporate the right services into a Go-to-Market Strategy tailored to each particular business environment.

CREATING SERVICE SUCCESS STORIES

While none of the business environments discussed above are more important than others, our experience with a variety of business-to-business suppliers has provided two important—and almost universal—services lessons. First, look for opportunities to define and deliver services that help customers increase sales. Second, look for opportunities to use advanced technologies and business systems to help customers and suppliers eliminate costs.

These lessons emerged from our research. In interviews that focused on services, we asked customers to describe a supplier success story. Almost all the success stories involved these two categories of services.

The first group of service-related success stories showed how the supplier helped its direct customers more effectively sell to and serve the end customers—and thereby grow their businesses. Some suppliers uncovered new ways of helping their customers use their products. In one instance, a supplier trained its sales representatives not only to restock shelves and calculate inventory needs at each of its direct customers' big-box locations, but also to discuss the technical trade-offs of the products with the end customer who was in the aisle, looking for assistance. Other suppliers provided educational and support services that contributed to productivity, using both traditional print media and new Internet channels. For example, food distributors hired chefs to develop precooked meals and then meet with restaurant customers to demonstrate the preparation techniques. One supplier uncovered a way of resolving a complex environmental challenge and incorporated this as a service surrounding its product. Still another supplier conducted market research and eventually reconfigured its product to help one of its major customers enter into a new global market and reach a cluster of end customers. All these services created value for the direct customer by increasing sales. And in every instance, the supplier captured value by enjoying increased sales as well.

When these customers described their supplier success stories, they told of suppliers that had listened closely to the needs of their end customers (reflecting an investment in knowledge), that had identified resourceful ways of creating value for these end customers (reflecting an investment in innovation and development), and that had composed a game plan along with their direct customers to get ahead of their competition (reflecting an ability to translate plans into action). These sales support services all were based on the suppliers' solid understanding of the critical success factors from the perspective of their targeted customer chain segments.

The second group of service-related success stories revealed how suppliers used advanced business systems, e-commerce strategies, and new technology to strengthen the supplier-customer connection. These stories underscored two themes that are relevant to service and e-service strategies: Understand the touch points between the supplier and its direct customer (or sales channel partner), and reshape the roles of and the boundaries between the two organizations. For example, a supplier of plumbing products started a technical chat room on its website where plumbers could share information and swap stories about difficult work tasks. The supplier then used this real-time market intelligence to fuel new product development and to build a list of plumbing contractors—cataloging areas of interest to identify potential early adopters of the new products. In another example, a supplier of building controls worked with its customers' maintenance staffs to remotely monitor facilities; they ensured that lights were turned off in the parking lot after hours, that doorways were closed, and that the air-conditioning and heating systems were working properly across the facility zones. These high levels of involvement across various functional groups were cited regularly as the success stories emerged. The touch points between suppliers and their customers are many and complex, particularly as relationships evolve. Best-in-class suppliers are thought of by their customers as careful students of these touch points, adept at aligning the two organizations along mutual interests and goals.

New technologies, often included under the e-commerce umbrella, were typically identified as the centerpiece of the supplier's contribution. Customers' examples all involved shifting technological roles and the blurring of organizational boundaries. One supplier posted technical information about upcoming product releases on its dealer website; this helped its channel partners quickly and competently respond to end customers' basic questions. Once the channel partner was empowered to directly address end customers' questions, the supplier's technical support personnel were free to field more sophisticated, complex questions. In this instance, the supplier delivered services to its channel partner that improved efficiency and productivity (for both itself and its sales channel partner) by using technology, new business systems, and innovative processes.

Much of the customers' praise of innovative service contributions involved suppliers that redefined the roles of the two organizations. One success story told of a livestock feed grain supplier that took on the responsibility for monitoring its major customer's feed inventories. The supplier placed a remote satellite–linked Web camera into the storage bins, so it could quickly determine whether to increase or decrease grain fulfillment levels. This supplier took ownership of the job to make sure there were no inventory shortfalls. Its approach not only built more accurate inventory information, but also allowed the customer to eliminate certain tasks. Supplier success stories within this category spanned a wide range of benefits to their customers: better, cheaper, faster—and frequently all three at once.

Less frequent, but of more significance to some customers, were examples in which advanced business systems and e-commerce strategies blurred the boundaries between the two organizations. Some cited effective information systems that brought new, high-impact insights to the customer organization; one case saw a dramatic improvement in forecasting and operational management, as in the feed grain example. Other customers cited the transformation of processes and linkages; one supplier-customer team had whittled an eight-step process down to a single step. As new approaches were defined and implemented, some suppliers were able to accomplish wholesale elimination of tasks (such as quality assurance and environmental compliance) that previously took up too much time and resources of both organizations.

Success in making services an effective component of an overall Go-to-Market Strategy, one that contributes to growth and profits, requires that the supplier both understand the complex customer chains that exist within its markets and accept the reality of the four distinct business environments within which it must operate.

Across the Market Map, the role played by support services varies considerably. The supplier must understand the environment in which each customer or cluster of customers is located, and must tailor its services strategy accordingly. Service strategies must complement the supplier's overall strategy in the four business environments while also responding to the customer's critical success factors, making distinctions across these environments.

Within this overall approach, the supplier should look carefully for ways to create and capture value through services strategies that strengthen its image as an innovator. Initiatives that foster win-win-win outcomes for customer chain segments within the lower left quadrant—or business systems and service initiatives that create value by changing the roles of and the boundaries between the supplier and its customers—are the most constructive alternatives within reach.

We fall mostly on the side of the executives at the lunch table who told service success stories—the right services tailored to the right customers can help a firm differentiate its position. But like the more familiar spectrum of Good-Better-Best that exists on the product spectrum, not all services are appropriate for all audiences. It's all a matter of listening to the messages from the market about the sources of value associated with services, and responding accordingly.

Chapter 11

TACKLE PRICING CHALLENGES

Many of our clients, and most firms in general, operate under tremendous pricing pressures. The harsh reality is that you must consider your company's pricing strategy very carefully, even if your product is offered in a less cutthroat environment where customers are focused on other factors. Pricing is always crucial in creating an effective Go-to-Market Strategy. It is always the element of strategy that first comes under assault by competitors—and often by customers.

One client learned that a competitor had delivered proposals to three of its largest accounts, offering to buy the business with incredibly aggressive pricing. Not surprisingly, these three customers asked our client for a response. The supplier-customer relationship with one of these customers, a longtime account, was very strong and seemed secure. The strategic account manager who worked with this customer obtained joint agreement to bring together teams from the two organizations; the goal was to define cost-saving ideas that would yield, at a minimum, the same bottom-line benefits promised by the competitor's proposal. Two meetings were held—one at a supplier facility and one at the customer's largest factory. The working teams developed seventeen action plans to reduce costs through collaboration and the redefinition of the two firms' roles and boundaries. About half of these ideas were unique to the businesses involved and the product lines sold by the supplier to this customer. The remaining ideas could be applied in many other settings, as suggested by the examples in figure 11.1.

The ideas developed by these teams were given a sharp-pencil review, especially in terms of feasibility: Was implementation practical? The outcome was a major win. This collaborative effort identified cost savings that far exceeded the price cuts offered by the competitor—in fact, both firms achieved margin improvements as a result of the process.

Our client tried to take this same concept to the other two firms that had entertained price-based competitive challenges. These were relatively new customers, and the supplier-customer relationships were largely transactional. In one case, the customer rejected the concept and gave the supplier two weeks to match the market or lose the business. Our client decided to restructure the contract with this customer, and while the business was retained, the attractiveness of this business relationship was substantially reduced as the supplier's margins dropped below acceptable levels. In the second case, the customer agreed to try the concept, but the two teams failed to get beyond sparring with one another about service and delivery issues. In the end, they could not agree on any action plans, and the supplier lost this business to its competition.

The latter two situations reflect the vicious cycle of pricing that compels so many business-to-business suppliers, as illustrated in figure 11.2. In this vicious cycle, one round of price-based competition invites the next. The pressures of this cutthroat environment make it less and

Figure 11.1: Supplier-Customer Action Plans

Cost Reduction Action Plans	
Coordinated Logistics	Eliminate empty backhauls associated with about 30 percent of the supplier deliveries to two of the customer's facilities.
Transparent Customer Service	Eliminate an estimated two person-years of effort spent in asking and answering questions about order status and delivery by giving the customer access to the supplier's service system.
Supplier-Provided Maintenance	Have supplier personnel at four facilities do routine, preventive, and corrective maintenance on equipment used by the customer, eliminating the need for a third-party maintenance contract.
Standardization of Installed Systems	Ensure that all the customer facilities use the same generation of the supplier's systems, reducing parts inventories by more than 20 percent and streamlining service operations.
Coordinated Forecasts	Link inventory management systems to provide near real-time information on demand, projected to reduce necessary safety stock levels by 8 percent.
One-Look Quality Control	Integrate the two companies' processes to avoid duplication and back-and-forth debates associated with product acceptance, reducing costs in this area by nearly 35 percent.

Figure 11.2: Vicious Cycle of Pricing

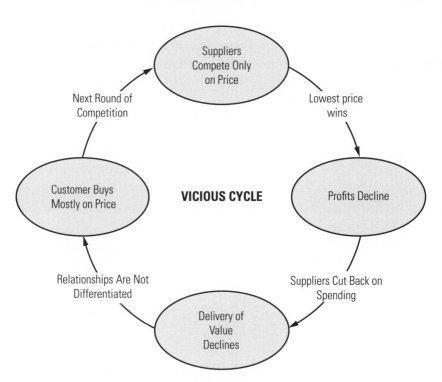

less likely that at each stage the downward spiral can be halted. The actions taken in this environment are all too familiar to many suppliers trapped within the cycle: Reduce spending on product development. Eliminate services. Pressure channel partners to accept lower margins (leading them, in turn, to eliminate services). Cut back on account management and customer service organizations. Face redirection of customers' resources to new markets. Neglect the supplier's brand. What is especially damaging in this cycle is the ongoing reductions in spending on products and services—areas that have the potential to break the cycle by adding value and differentiating a firm's position. Such cutbacks drive the firms in the industry to an undifferentiated commodity position. And in that situation, when the offerings of various suppliers are largely the same, customers are right in making their purchase decisions mostly based on price.

Fortunately, suppliers rarely have to compete for customers on price alone, as illustrated by the supplier's success with the first customer and by many of the examples in previous chapters. And when they do, strong customer relationships—the Relationship Advantage—often can defend against price-based competition. But the lessons from the case history go far beyond this.

PRICE IS ALWAYS IMPORTANT

First, price is always important. It will always be a visible and important part of the business relationship between a supplier and a customer. An important part of the long-term plan for a customer relationship must always center on pricing. Stronger customer relationships do not make price disappear from the decision calculus. Rather, such relationships provide an opportunity to address the importance of price in a constructive fashion, as part of the relationship strategy.

Furthermore, as was the situation in this case study, competitive challenges frequently begin with an offer of lower prices, with competitors trying to buy the business. So suppliers must always be prepared to contend with these aggressive approaches, regardless of how secure they are in their Relationship Advantage. But lower prices need not always trigger price concessions. In the next chapter, we'll see how a firm can evaluate the level of threat posed by various competitive challenges, including ones involving lower prices. Sometimes price-based challenges are a real threat, but not always.

It is critical that firms look at the Market Map to understand how pricing fits into their overall strategy and position. The quadrant location of the customer business is a key indicator of the role of pricing vis-à-vis the other elements of a Go-to-Market Strategy. For a firm in the upper right quadrant, lower prices are a material threat. If a competitor can meet the customer's specifications at a lower price point, it is likely that they will win the business. In that environment, the mandate is to achieve a low-cost position. This will allow the supplier to prevent competitors from creating value for the customer by offering a lower price (and still capturing greater value for themselves with this new business). By contrast, in the lower left quadrant, a firm with a superior offering in terms of the key product and service decision drivers can command a price premium.

In the two off-diagonal quadrants where direct and end customer purchase decisions are not well aligned, pricing pressures must again be taken seriously. In the upper left quadrant, unless the supplier can marshal end customer pull for its product, it will see direct customers taking lower-price offers quite seriously. If the supplier's business isn't one where the end customer demands the supplier's product, the direct customer's preferences win the day, and the mandate to achieve a low-cost position is basically the same as in the upper right quadrant's business environment. Similarly, in the lower right quadrant, with end customers putting price pressure on the direct customer, these pressures can be passed back along the customer chain to the supplier. Here, however, the supplier often has options that can be more attractive to its customer than lower prices, as with our client whose seventeen cost-reducing action plans saved the day.

ANTICIPATING AND ADDRESSING PRICE PRESSURES

The importance of understanding the pricing environment cannot be understated. Today's firms find themselves operating in business environments that require them to take lower competitive prices as a serious threat. After reviewing the Market Map to decide on an overall strategy, suppliers must also take a second step: Assess the degree to which pricing pressures are likely to emerge.

We've identified four categories of factors that are often useful in predicting pricing pressures. The first of these involves capacity utilization in both the suppliers' and the customers' industries. When, in either case, there is considerable excess capacity, pricing pressures are likely to emerge. The second category involves various forms of protection— from formal, legal factors (e.g., patents, government-granted monopoly powers) to cost-prohibitive factors (e.g., capital investments, research and development requirements)—that build a barrier to competitive entry, reducing the threat of price pressures. The third set of factors reflects the business environment: When markets are strong and growing, when end product values are high, and when an offering involves a solution or a complex process, pricing pressures are less likely. Finally, as we discussed in chapter 8, pricing pressures are likely to be less of a challenge when relationships are strong, when they're centered on technical or marketing interaction (rather than purchasing alone), and when the supplier's contributions to its customer's products are significant and visible.

These four factors can help a supplier assess the likelihood that the firm will face pricing pressures. When the assessment suggests that price pressures are a possibility, it provides the firm with advance warning. It then has the opportunity to be proactive in developing its position and its response to price-based challenges.

Our research into business strategy has identified distinct approaches that a supplier can use to address pricing challenges. One such approach follows on the case study above: Identify and implement action plans to "take costs out of the system" through supplier-customer collaboration and via shifts in their roles and boundaries. This strategy successfully removes costs from the equation by pushing the focus of value creation away from pricing and toward other areas of mutual benefit. You can't just wish pricing challenges away, but you can refocus the customer's attention on other approaches to value creation. And while our client in this chapter's case study used the strategy after the fact to blunt a price challenge, we've seen this approach used proactively with great success, to preempt future pricing problems.

So while price is always important, there are ways to mitigate its effect on your standing with business customers. The second lesson that emerges from the earlier case study is that relationships, not just products, can be differentiated. This statement—an obvious truth to some managers—has been overlooked by many organizations as a whole. Once again we are forced to note that strong relationships don't eliminate the importance of pricing—or the customer's focus on it. They can, however, enhance a firm's ability to offer its customers alternative sources of value creation as part of an effective Go-to-Market Strategy.

Relationship differentiation is an ongoing process, an endless racetrack that requires the runners to continually focus on opportunities for value creation. The supplier must pay constant attention to the next prospect for creating and capturing value; it must constantly invest in the actions necessary to take advantage of these opportunities. Many firms that achieve differentiated status are able to realize premium prices only occasionally. Instead, differentiation more often leads to a share premium and to a more secure, growing relationship. In fact, it is our belief that to avoid the vicious cycle of pricing, gain a share premium, and maintain stable customer relationships is an extraordinary achievement for a supplier. Moreover, in even the best situations, premium prices are transitory phenomena, and suppliers must be careful that the transition from premium prices to market prices does not become the first step toward ruinous price competition.

In the course of our work, one supplier recognized that its most profitable business was located in the lower left quadrant of the Market Map. As its technology was maturing, however, the firm's leadership saw price pressures emerging as competitors began to close the gap. The supplier did a careful analysis of its position, calculating the percentage gain in volume that would compensate for price reductions. It identified a new product application under development by one of its key customers that could yield a more than 20 percent increase in business. By proactively offering a price reduction consistent with its calculations, the supplier was able to secure this business. In doing so, it preempted major pricing pressures on its existing business, and also established a foundation to later drive this product onto additional platforms with this customer.

Suppliers have used other strategies to manage price competition. One client with a strong track record requires that a value engineering plan be developed internally before contracts are signed. This organization enters a new customer relationship with both a celebration of the contract it has won and a plan to manage the price path over the life of that contract. This supplier explained, "We woke up when we saw that we *always* had to develop a crisis plan around pricing. We go much further when we initiate the discussions instead of having to answer the mail."

A second supplier requires that its global customer teams develop an annual plan for each overall relationship. This goes considerably beyond the elements of a typical sales plan, with this firm's plan including assessments of where the firm intends to invest in the relationship, what expectations it has in terms of supplier-led initiatives, what gaps it hopes to fill in the relationship, where it expects pricing pressures, and so on. A senior executive in this organization noted, "We get an A for continuing to strengthen our key major customer relationships, year after year, just about without fail. We get a B or a B- for anticipating problems and getting ahead of them—but that might be the highest grade in the class, so we know this effort is worth the time and energy that it takes."

A third supplier has invested in several competitive simulations that give structured assessments of how other firms might make a grab for its business. In the eyes of this organization, the effort has injected more realism into its business plans. One executive explained, "The pain from price pressures comes when the annual plan doesn't include them. So when they come, and they inevitably do come, they put you into a hole that you can't dig out of. By making a conscious effort to see what is in store for us, we can bake some realism into the annual plans, as well as try to head off the most disastrous situations at the pass."

CREATING A WIN FOR CUSTOMERS

One important step to successfully becoming proactive on pricing is to have an explicit notion of what "win-win" might mean, both across the customer relationship and in the context of the relationship within each of its specific segments. Customers can always define one win that creates value for them: lower prices offered by their suppliers. In turn, the supplier's challenge is to showcase an alternative that the customer comes to see as a better approach to value creation.

Many best-in-class suppliers have a clear understanding of what a win would be for their own organizations. Sometimes the supplier's win is higher volume, whether in the current segments where it supplies its customers or in new segments associated with new markets or customers' growth plans. Sometimes the supplier's win is higher margins through successful value engineering programs in collaboration with the customer. Sometimes the supplier's win is a longer, more stable relationship that requires lower costs to serve and lower costs to sell. In any case, a clear definition of what a win might mean can lead to a proactive approach by the supplier to steer the relationship toward that outcome.

Fundamental to this value capture strategy, however, is understanding how the customer can achieve a win. Best-in-class suppliers gain considerable insight from their efforts to put themselves in their customers' shoes to define what a win might mean to them. In a number of cases, we've worked with suppliers to construct alternative portraits of a customer win; we've put equally great efforts into the plan for communicating these portraits to their customers. To get to this vantage point, the supplier must understand the economic foundations of the supplier-customer relationship. From that understanding, it can develop initiatives that are win-win.

Suppliers must go into this process knowing that the climb is uphill; success will require both creativity and a proactive stance. They must overcome the unfortunate starting point, where many major customers' portrait of a win involves lower prices from their suppliers. The customer's purchasing organization (and in fact, most supply chain management approaches) is prone to viewing production in terms of input-output processes: The customer's goal is to procure the necessary inputs, according to a well-defined set of specs, at minimum cost. This perspective offers the supplier few opportunities for differentiation or value creation, and in some sense, that is the goal of many approaches to supply chain management: to foster price-based competition among as many suppliers as possible.

Our perspective differs. As we revealed in chapter 5, we recognize that suppliers have three ways to create a win for their customers: They can help customers increase market share, increase prices, or cut costs. When the supplier doesn't or can't contribute in one of these three ways, it should expect pricing pressures, and should recognize that its only real contribution to the customer is its ability to meet specs at minimum cost. We continue to deliver the positive message of creating value for your customers in order to capture value for your shareholders, but the corollary message is much more harsh: If you can't create value for your customers, don't expect to be able to capture value for your shareholders. Expect, instead, to live in a world defined by the vicious price cycle.

The vast majority of suppliers, however, can and do contribute along one or more of these three dimensions of value creation. A strong Go-to-Market Strategy builds from the supplier's careful assessment of how to contribute along each dimension. The way to start this assessment is to measure what is actually required in terms of the economic relationships specific to each product and market segment. It is instructive to review the three value creation options: What must be done? What will be achieved? What must be sold to the customer?

The first win requires that the supplier present a value proposition to the targeted customer, saying, "Inclusion of our products will help you gain market share." With the customer facing market prices for its products, its revenues are fixed; it believes that its profitability will be higher with a lower-priced product. However, if end customers recognize the superiority of the supplier's products and reward the direct customer with stronger market share, in fact the customer can be better off.

To back this claim of helping the customer gain market share, the supplier will likely have to deliver product enhancements or surrounding services; this will ensure that its brand is the end customer's preference and, in the best of situations, also the direct customer's. Suppliers that have succeeded with this strategy typically have a strong sense of both the factors that promote satisfaction among end customers and the factors that offer perceived advantages to direct customers.

The second possible win for the supplier relies on the major customer's ability to charge a premium price for its products without losing market share. If the direct customer is able to at least pass along the higher price from the supplier—to those end customers who feel that the direct customer's product benefits from inclusion of the supplier's product—the direct customer can remain whole or even increase profits by marking up the supplier's product. The initial reaction of many suppliers to this concept is "Not in my lifetime will I see a customer buy into this." Yet the truth is, numerous items are standard today that were never part of yesterday's generation of products until the direct customers learned that end customers would pay handsome prices for those features.

Each of us, in our personal and business lives, can quickly think of examples where we selected an optional feature at a higher price because, in some way, we considered it worth the extra money. In fact, one approach to gaining agreement from a direct customer about including a higher-priced ingredient is to offer it as an option to end customers. When the option is selected frequently by the end customers, the supplier has the optimal proof statement that its contribution created value by helping the direct customer reach a higher price point. In a number of instances that we've observed, the option that was frequently selected by end customers eventually evolved to become part of the standard offering from the supplier's direct customer.

In this win category, the supplier must prove its case to the direct customer. If the supplier's differentiation is not meaningful to end customers, there is no reason to expect that either the direct customer or the end customer would pay a higher price. On the other hand, if there is truly a value-added differential, both the supplier and the direct customer can be rewarded for the product's superiority.

The supplier's third option for presenting a win to targeted customers requires the value proposition "Inclusion of our products will save you money in other areas." To back this claim, the supplier likely will have to showcase design, engineering, new materials, business systems, or other initiatives that take costs out of the total system. Even if improved products or surrounding services cost more per unit than do offerings from the supplier's competitors, direct customers can remain whole or see profit improvements if they see cost savings in other categories. The supplier could be rewarded by higher margins, increased sales, or strengthened long-term relationships with direct customers that appreciate the "total systems" perspective. Or it could reap a combination of these benefits.

In working with one supplier, we developed a detailed analysis of its economic relationship with one key customer to whom it sold a number of products and modules for a particular application. We developed estimates of what the direct customer would have to realize in order to justify paying this supplier 3 percent more than it paid a competitor. In addition to looking at the direct customer's price and market share with respect to end customers, we also considered the cost environment (the relevant manufacturing, warranty, and other costs) associated with each product or module.

Two of our client's offerings differed in how they might create value, and thus in how our client analyzed and presented them. Module A was considered to be largely invisible to end customers in terms of performance or other attributes, so it was implausible that the supplier would be able to position its Better product to yield market share gains or a price premium. On the other hand, the cost reductions in adjacent products and assembly that would be required to offset a 3 percent price premium were very small—just over 0.6 percent of those adjacent costs. For module B, the cost reductions required to offset the same 3 percent price differential were enormous—nearly 20 percent of the estimated adjacent costs incurred by this customer. On the other hand, this module was quite visible to end customers—an important part of a key driver of customer satisfaction. It was quite plausible to argue that the superior product offered by this supplier should yield sales of about 775 extra units, or a price premium of $66 on a five-figure product.

To introduce these two different module strategies, the supplier had to address different customer touch points, building upon its overall management of this customer relationship. For module A, with a focus on removing costs from the system, the critical touch points involved the design, manufacturing, and logistics connections between the two companies. For module B, with a focus on end customer satisfaction and selling more units, the connections to the customer's marketing and sales organizations were important, as were those with the advanced engineering group that would ratify the supplier's claim of technical superiority over the competition.

This short example points to the importance of an effective Go-to-Market Strategy that ensures consistency across all of its elements. This allows the firm to both manage the pricing dimensions of a relationship and refocus discussions on other approaches to value creation. By broadening the scope of the value proposition, the supplier can shift the ratification process outside the customer's purchasing organization, since the justifications depend so heavily on helping the customer succeed with its end customers or achieve productivity gains in other areas of their operations.

Business-to-business suppliers know that pricing is among their most significant and important responsibilities. Price pressures and the impact these pressures have on profits increase with the size of the customer relationship, as does the incentive for competitors to try to win the account through lower prices. Suppliers simply must take proactive steps to avoid the vicious price cycle, to refocus customer attention on their other contributions to value creation, and to ensure that customers continue to prop up the suppliers' own growth and profitability. These steps include formally making cost-cutting action plans a part of the Go-to-Market Strategy and continually searching for value creation opportunities that can differentiate the relationship.

Chapter 12

CONFRONT YOUR COMPETITIVE CHALLENGES

Transforming the business relationship from one defined by price battles into one that makes your customers *want* to pay more for your product requires your ongoing focus and effort. The previous chapter identified ways for an organization to refocus discussions with its customers on opportunities for value creation rather than price reduction. Like the reality of pricing discussions in business relationships, there is an ongoing reality of competitor challenges that business firms must recognize and confront. As this chapter reveals, an exploration of the primary opportunities for value creation also provides insights about the seriousness of competitor threats and the strategies most likely to thwart them.

As we mentioned earlier, suppliers have three primary options for differentiation in their business relationships:

1. **Product and service advantages**—offer superior products and services.

2. **Cost advantages**—offer lower price points.

3. **Relationship Advantages**—build a superior business relationship.

By superimposing these three options against the Market Map concepts, suppliers can plan a competitive response that protects the firm's base business and encourages growth.

Chapter 6 describes the behavioral segments that exist in most business markets, according to the factors that drive purchase decision making at each stage of the customer chain. The four business environments—the four quadrants of the Market Map—are shown as the rows in figure 12.1. The columns reflect the three options for differentiation, and the cell entries offer a capsule evaluation of each option.

PLANNING TO COMPETE

Suppliers can use this assessment to plan their competitive response; it also offers some positive insights about how to stay ahead of the competition and avoid pressures on prices. Note that the three competitive options vary widely across the four business environments in terms of importance. As a consequence, the nature of the most severe competitive threat and the optimal response—whether reactive or proactive—also varies from one environment to the next.

The upper right quadrant, in which both direct and end customers are highly price sensitive, is the one environment where the supplier's primary competitive option is to offer a lower price. Competitors that bring lower prices to customers are a significant threat in this

Figure 12.1: Differentiation Options in Four Business Environments

	Superior Product and Service Offering	Lower Price Point	Superior Relationship
Upper Right Quadrant: Direct and End Customers Are Both Focused on Price	Likely to be embraced only if they don't involve higher prices.	Lower prices along this dimension win in this environment.	Difficult to sustain with customers who are constantly looking for better prices.
Lower Right Quadrant: End Customers Are Focused on Price, with Direct Customers Considering Non-Price Factors	If superior product and service contributions can be made without a major price impact, this may help the direct customer win on a tiebreaker basis.	Lower prices aren't material enough to carry the day in the end market, but would clearly be accepted by the direct customer.	Strong relationships are likely to be prerequisite in order to bring innovations that take costs out by changing the roles of and the boundaries between suppliers and their direct customers.
Upper Left Quadrant: End Customer Are Focused on Non-price Factors, But Direct Customers Emphasize Price	Product and service advantages may help to create pull-through demand from end customers, but higher prices associated with these contributions will be resisted by the direct customer.	Lower prices are likely to be applauded by the direct customer.	Relationships with direct customers may be difficult to establish given their price focus. Relationships with end customers may help drive pull-through demand.
Lower Left Quadrant: Both Direct and End Customers Are Focused on Non-price Factors	Product and service advantages win in this environment.	No one rejects lower prices, but this is not the critical factor in this environment.	Stronger relationships may pave the way for innovation and solutions.

environment, and it is unrealistic to expect to avoid a focus on price. It is in this market environment that we most often see vicious cycles of lower and lower price-based competition. Ultimately, long-term success belongs to the firms with superior cost structures, in their own operations and in their supply bases. Lessons from this environment, however, do not apply in the other three environments. Firms that choose price-based competition as their standard mode of behavior often miss the best opportunities to create value for their customers and capture it for their shareholders.

In the lower right quadrant, end customers focus largely on price, but direct customers tend to focus more on other factors (often because the supplier's prices don't "move the needle" in terms of their own cost structure). This market bears the closest resemblance to the upper right quadrant. As we discussed earlier, superior product and service offerings can be argued on the basis of a tiebreaker contribution, but direct customers typically resist paying more to suppliers when their own customers are unlikely to allow them to pass along these higher prices. So from the supplier's perspective, superior product and service offerings are a competitive threat or an effective competitive response only when they can be delivered at unchanged prices. Lower prices, on the other hand, are welcomed, and direct customers are likely to focus on this when they communicate with suppliers. Suppliers in this environment must work to avoid becoming caught in a vicious pricing cycle to have any chance of success. Lower prices don't really create much value for their direct customers in the greater scheme of things.

Instead of lower prices, there exists in this environment the possibility for new contributions to bring innovative approaches to take cost out of the supplier-customer system and create savings. In chapter

8, we emphasized the Relationship Advantage as the primary competitive option in this environment, at least for firms that can identify and implement actions that take costs out of the combined supplier-customer system to thwart competitive efforts based on price. This non-priced-based approach in the lower right quadrant allows both the supplier and the customer to gain from a similar destiny. The customers that embrace these ideas can realize major savings benefits, and at the same time, the supplier's relationship with them can be cemented to a point where competitive approaches based on lower product prices are dismissible. This non-price-based competitive response that a supplier implements can be far more appropriate, and far more effective, than any effort to respond to the lower price points proposed by its competitors.

The upper left quadrant—where the end customers focus on factors other than price and direct customers emphasize price in their buying behavior—also invites competitive challenges. Competing along the price dimension alone in this environment is likely to initiate a vicious cycle, to the detriment of the suppliers involved in the competition.

As we have stressed, one of the prerequisites for this type of strategy is end customer visibility of the supplier's contribution and end customer recognition of the importance of the supplier's product. We have also observed numerous instances of this business environment when the customer chains involve channel organizations, such as distributors, wholesalers, integrators, and dealers. Channel organizations frequently carry a wide spectrum of products, many of which are undifferentiated from one manufacturer to another. Furthermore, they often operate in an intensely competitive arena where they face a variety of competitors. Thus, to a significant extent, the overall business environment seen by these channel organizations is much like the upper right quadrant. For some product lines, however, end customers may see strong differentiation between manufacturers. As a result, the manufacturers involved in these customer chains also face business environments similar to the upper left quadrant.

Our research into strategy in such situations has yielded the development of what we call "Supplier Driven business models," which are oriented toward creating a win for each participant along the customer chains involved.[13] The concept of the Supplier Driven business model is straightforward: Both the manufacturer and the channel organization have unique, important roles to play in meeting the end customer's requirements—unlike the situation in the Channel Driven business model, where the manufacturer rarely interacts with the end customer. For manufacturers that go to market through channel relationships within the upper left quadrant, this business model prescribes a strategy of building relationships at the end customer stage, providing the basis for competitive and bottom-line success. We'll return in chapter 15 to a discussion of strategies for value creation and capture for firms that go to market through third-party channels.

In the fourth business environment, the lower left quadrant, both direct customers and end customers emphasize factors other than price in their purchasing behavior. This environment can be as intensely competitive as any of the others, but as figure 12.1 suggests, the basis of competition shifts away from price and toward themes of product, service, and technology. In this business market, the most challenging

---

13. Atlee Valentine Pope and George F. Brown, Jr., *"Supplier Driven" and "Channel Driven" Business Models* (Evanston, IL: Blue Canyon Partners, Inc., 2006).

threat involves the better mousetrap. When price-based competition evolves in this environment, it usually is a signal that the industry has become stale and has failed to advance its contributions.

We have mentioned being told by clients that they run price-based competitions only because "all the suppliers are the same, with none of them bringing anything new or better to the table." These same customers are typically able to provide a clear roster of desired improvements in the products and services they seek from one of those competitors. When suppliers fail to respond to the value creation opportunities volunteered by their own customers, the lower-left-quadrant environment is essentially transformed into an upper right quadrant.

GETTING AHEAD OF COMPETITION

Charlie Peters, Senior Executive Vice President of Emerson, developed a wonderful case study that challenged students in the company's education programs to assess the competitive threats facing the various divisions of a company and to develop competitive responses to those challenges.[14] As the student works through this case, he or she discovers that some threats are more real than others, and that the responses to the most genuine threats demand different reactions and competencies. This case study mirrors the real world of competition, where not every threat involves lower prices and not every reaction requires cutting prices. The lesson of planning to compete is one that can help most firms grow in new markets even as they protect their positions and margins in the markets they already serve.

---

14. Charles A. Peters, *Mann Metes Match* (Emerson Corporate University case study, 2006).

A firm that is proactive in diagnosing real threats and presenting competitive options is way ahead of the game, compared to one that must always react to competitor actions. Building a higher-level relationship with a direct customer opens the door for game-changing innovations, and building a higher-level relationship with an end customer presents the possibility of developing pull-through demand, but these types of relationship building take time, effort, and great insight. Best-practice firms recognize early on the most challenging threats in each of the market segments they inhabit and, from the beginning, work on the competitive responses that will create value for their customers, thwarting those threats.

Chapter 13

CREATE VALUE THROUGH ACQUISITIONS

Decisions concerning acquisitions, joint ventures, and other such partnering arrangements are an important component of an effective Go-to-Market Strategy. Such initiatives can in fact yield value for shareholders, but all too often they fail to do so. Many firms report that this is partly because their acquisitions come with unforeseen demands that consume valuable time and resources. Yet we're convinced that business leaders who build acquisition processes from a framework of value creation are the best prepared to achieve success. Within this framework, acquisition options are evaluated from the perspective of their contribution to the firm's strategy. Making sure that the acquisition candidate or the prospective partner is truly going to mesh with the firm's approach to value creation can mean all the difference.

More than fifty years ago, Igor Ansoff developed a framework for thinking about acquisitions, focusing on four reasons a company might consider this avenue: share gain, new market entry, new product development, and diversification.[15] Ansoff emphasized the increased level of difficulty that exists when a firm moves away from its current

15. Igor Ansoff, "Strategies for Diversification," *Harvard Business Review* (September-October 1957).

markets and its current products, with the greatest degree of difficulty existing when it attempts to do both at once. Most firms today have processes in place designed to examine acquisition opportunities from this perspective, and the Ansoff Matrix is a staple in many of the planning processes of leading businesses around the globe.

But our research has led us to an intriguing conclusion: Many acquisition failures involved a failure to effectively implement Ansoff's ideas. Too many business leaders look at an acquisition from a demographic perspective rather than a behavioral perspective.[16] With careful analysis of the customer chain and the Market Map, however, acquisition decisions can become an important part of a successful Go-to-Market Strategy, as illustrated in the following case studies.

The first case study involves a leading tool manufacturer whose products were viewed as "the ones to own" by the mechanics and craftsmen in its customer base. Its market share was impressive, but this was a crowded industry with numerous competitors and diverse offerings. When another tool company serving the same vertical segments presented itself to this firm, it looked like an ideal acquisition opportunity within the easiest quadrant of the Ansoff Matrix: current products sold to current customers. This "short putt," as it was described by one company leader, turned into a double bogey.

Figure 13.1 provides insight on why this turned into a horror story. This company's core business had channel partners as direct customers and mechanics and craftsmen as end customers. At both stages of the customer chain, purchase decisions were driven by quality and service rather than price. Channel partners made most of their income

---

16. Atlee Valentine Pope and George F. Brown, Jr., *Five Growth Lessons* (Evanston, IL: Blue Canyon Partners, Inc., 2008).

Figure 13.1: Tool Manufacturing Acquisition Market Map

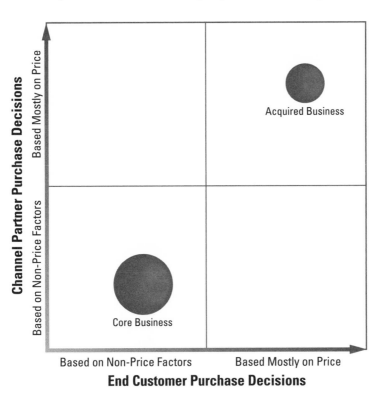

from services; they looked to this manufacturer for its brand reputation and its ability to attract the premier customers. End customers were looking for top-of-the-line tools and the highest possible levels of support, and they were willing to pay for these items. The company's Core Business bubble is thus solidly in the lower left quadrant of the diagram, where purchase decisions at both stages of the customer chain are driven mainly by factors other than price.

The firm then considered the buying behavior of the new business's customers. As it turned out, the acquired company—while offering products whose names were the same as those offered by the core company and which were sold to end customers who also described themselves as mechanics and craftsmen—served quite a different segment. Its channel partners subscribed to the "stack 'em high and watch 'em fly" theory (as one client described it), with services that would be called bare-bones by even the most generous observers. In fact, about half of the supplier's volume came from manufacturing private-label brands for channel organizations that needed to include a "price buy" among their offerings. The end customers served through these channels were always looking for low prices, and they worked aggressively to find them.

It soon became apparent that this acquisition was in fact squarely in a different quadrant of the Ansoff Matrix than expected: new products to new customers, the most challenging possible combination.

First, the company thought it could achieve some economies of scale through careful purchasing and management of the supply chain. Due to the nature of the acquirer-acquiree structure and to the relative scale of the two firms, the core business's supply chain emerged as the winner. Unfortunately, even after some scale-driven gains that actually exceeded the pre-acquisition forecast, the costs of using these suppliers averaged 20 percent higher than the acquired company was accustomed to. As a result, while the core business benefited in terms of margin improvement, the acquired business suffered a significant blow to its competitiveness.

Second, the acquiring firm proudly implemented its processes for manufacturing optimization and inventory management, which it had long linked to its successes. While these processes were in many ways best-in-class and a source of value within its own customer chains, they were a burden to the acquired company. In the words of a former executive of the acquired company, "A costly albatross hung around our neck as we were thrown overboard." Once again, the acquired company's ability to compete in the markets in which it was positioned suffered badly.

An even bigger problem presented itself: a threat to the pride and careful stewardship long associated with the acquiring company's brand. For this firm, private labels were the enemy, and overtures coming from private-label manufacturers had long been given a speedy dismissal. After the integration of the newly acquired firm, this practice continued—even for some of the channel customers that previously had been served by the acquired firm as a contract manufacturer of their private-label products. In short order, nearly one-fourth of the pre-acquisition volume was lost. During this process, one key channel relationship was lost in its entirety, shifting its purchases to a firm willing to provide both branded and private-label products. Other channel relationships were harmed, although not to the same extent. Moreover, as volume dropped, the cost structure of the acquired firm once again shifted in the wrong direction for its end customers.

We've observed the same disappointment in other situations. For example, one company completed the acquisition of a Chinese vehicle parts manufacturer that was operating distinctly in the upper right quadrant. This Shanghai operation was modern, with headquarters centrally located in the advanced coastal region of China. It was quite capable of producing parts that met customer specifications, and it was succeeding due to a far lower cost structure than that of the acquiring company. Decision makers in the United States had been confident that the low labor costs of this Chinese acquisition would be a major boost to the bottom line, without compromising the firm's position as a leader in product quality and technology.

As it turned out, however, the cost structure of this modern operation was highly dependent on a set of small local suppliers in rural western China, where costs were a fraction of those in Shanghai. Once the acquisition process was complete and the acquired company was told to purchase only from the approved supplier list, the company began bleeding cash. The acquisition was turning into a major disappointment for the parent company. It wasn't even clear that the China operation, after transportation costs, could match the economics in the United States. Dramatic changes in the process of managing the supply chain dragged on so long that some reliable Chinese suppliers were lost, and relationships had to be rebuilt at great cost.

In addition to enforcing the approved supplier list, headquarters also explained to the Chinese executives that the Global Product Approval Center would play a crucial role in the new process. The GPAC would approve all new products before final release, requiring round after round of extensive testing. What the parent company failed to take into consideration, though, was that the market in China was moving at lightning speed. New product introductions by the firm's Chinese competitors averaged every three months—roughly half the time required for the GPAC to perform its first round of tests.

While it would be possible to extend the case studies of the tool manufacturer and the auto parts manufacturer for several more pages, the implications are clear. Acquisition decisions must be based on a clear analysis of the customer chain and purchase decision drivers if they are to contribute to an effective Go-to-Market Strategy.

The following case study provides another example of the challenges of acquisitions. As illustrated in figure 13.2, the acquiring firm had direct and end customers that emphasized factors other than price in their purchase decisions. Meanwhile, the firm that was acquired served segments in the lower right quadrant.

The acquired and acquiring firms in this case were ingredients suppliers; their customer chain involved a second-stage manufacturer that incorporated their ingredients into its end product, which was then sold to end customers. The direct customer's purchase decisions, in both cases, were largely driven by non-price factors, since the suppliers'

Figure 13.2: Acquisition Market Map

ingredients accounted for only a small fraction of the final product price, though they did matter to the end customers in terms of performance and reliability. The two firms reached end customer segments that were quite distinct from one another, however, with the acquirer's customer chains largely reaching the elite segments and the acquiree reaching price-conscious end customers.

The success that emerged in this case reflected one of the core competencies of the acquiring company, namely, that of being a great supplier to its customers. The firm's corporate ethic involved careful customer relationship management, intense listening to what mattered and what didn't, and meticulous follow-through. For the core business, this process had yielded a focus on new product development and innovation, and its direct customers credited this ingredient supplier with numerous successes that turned into growth for both participants.

When this supplier applied its great customer processes and listening skills to customers served by the newly acquired firm, it heard the market message loud and clear: New products and innovation just didn't matter very much. What did matter were ways to cut costs and improve productivity. The second-stage manufacturing customers that had been acquired were straightforward and eloquent about this priority. The acquiring firm heard the message, acted on it, and turned its considerable talents to the task of responding to these needs. It successfully identified ways to respond to the challenge of cutting costs and improving productivity, and revenues and profits from the acquired business's market segment grew rapidly.

This could have gone badly. Had the acquired firm indiscriminately transferred the sources of success in its core businesses to its new acquisition, the story would have been much like that of the tool company acquisition.

There is another important lesson to be learned from this case study. The acquiring firm had a long history of new product successes, and even measured its executives on the basis of revenues associated with newly launched products. After the acquisition, a human resources executive tried to implement standard measurement plans among the executives of the newly acquired company. It took a second iteration before the firm's leadership recognized that while new products were a key profit driver in the core businesses, longer product life cycles were in fact a key to success in the acquired business units. Considering the buying behavior of the market they served was essential not only to the customer-facing portions of the acquirer and the acquiree, but in fact to all the functions involved in the management of the business.

There are numerous potential combinations of "current" and "new" when purchase decision drivers are considered, but the assessment is well defined when a specific acquisition candidate is under consideration. Mapping the customer chains and purchase decision drivers of the acquiring company against those of the acquired company is a straightforward process. Thus the framework for understanding value creation can serve a company seeking to manage decisions about acquisitions. The framework encourages business leaders to consider the fundamental question: Will this new partnership capture value for shareholders?

The first phase of this process requires that the potential acquirer look carefully at the value creation environment for the acquisition candidate. What factors drive purchase decisions at each stage of the acquisition candidate's customer chain? Are these factors best characterized as "current" (being served by us already) or "new" (at least at some stage or stages of the customer chain)? Do our competencies complement and augment those of the potential acquisition?

When segments involve "new" purchase decision drivers, acquiring firms must ask whether they are prepared to manage a business that involves diversification and a new and unfamiliar approach to value creation: Can the acquired company bring us the needed competencies? Can we avoid destroying them during the acquisition process? Do we have any competencies that can take the performance of the acquired company to a higher level, and therefore justify an argument of synergy? Are the acquisition economies included in the business case (e.g., scale effects, supply base consolidation, process implementation) consistent with the actual mix of "current" and "new" segments that we serve and target? Or are we creating an unfounded business case by arguing that these businesses can be integrated without harming the ability of one or the other firm to maintain the successes it has achieved?

Figure 13.3 contains a summary of the elements at stake and the rationale that must be developed to ensure that strong value creation and value capture opportunities are in play.

Only by careful analysis of the relationships with customers, third-party channel intermediaries, and suppliers will a company be able to make successful acquisition decisions within the context of an overall Go-to-Market Strategy.

Figure 13.3: Acquisition Considerations

	Elements	Rationale
Strategic Intent	Objectives; sources of leverage; strategic benefits to acquiring company; expected results	Description of the contributions that the acquisition can make; overview of the short-term and medium-term impacts on growth and profitability
Source of Value Creation	Untapped business potential; revenue opportunities and synergies; cost synergies; added value for the marketplace	Areas of business improvements resulting from the new business model scenario, including increased revenues or savings; scenario assessment
Fit and Integration Scenario	Customer and channel partners; impact on key external relationships	Description of the proposed integration and assimilation of the new business, including impacts on and links to acquiring company's core competencies
Business Risks	Competitive impact; customer defection; operational problems; other inherent liabilities	Analysis of feasibility; competitor reactions; impacts of possible customer defections

Chapter 14

SELECT YOUR CUSTOMERS AND GROWTH MARKETS

One of our clients, having just completed a year defined by solid profitable growth, commented, "The smartest decision I made was picking the right customers." We generally concur with that comment, as successful years are almost always shared between suppliers and their customers.

Our first lesson when it comes to selecting customers is this: For many suppliers in business markets, the best growth prospects are the firm's current customers. While it can seem as though the grass is always greener on the other side—particularly when a company looks over the fence at fast-growing global markets—the best growth prospects, particularly in the short term, are there among your existing customers. This is especially true for firms that have built strong relationships with major customers and can leverage these relationships into new ways of delivering value. Over the years, in literally hundreds of projects involving growth strategy, it has been a rare instance indeed in which we could not identify solid growth prospects among the customers currently served by our clients. This does not detract from the ongoing challenge of finding interesting new markets and customers to serve, but it does define the first place to look for growth for most companies as they develop their Go-to-Market Strategy.

The second lesson about choosing customers for growth is this: It is much easier to sell into growth than to capture share from competitors. Almost always, the incumbent suppliers are doing many things well, so they have an advantage over any challenger trying to take their business. This does not mean displacing competitors is impossible, but simply that it is hard. We therefore look, as one indicator of the attractiveness of markets, at the available growth across market segments into which a firm can sell.

One client identified four potentially interesting target markets. Figure 14.1 shows each market's size expressed as the estimated annual units purchased (scale), and the compounded annual growth rate expected from these markets over a five-year forecast horizon (growth).

Markets A and B were unambiguously larger than Markets C and D, and would continue to be for five years. But these markets were mature, with very little year-over-year growth expected, particularly in Market A. By contrast, while Market D was the smallest of the four, it was projected to experience the greatest amount of growth over the forecast period, followed by Market C.

Identifying the best markets for a company to target is never simple, as both scale and growth are relevant. But ignoring the growth into which a company can sell is a mistake.

We went further in our analysis for this client. Through discussions in the marketplace, we were able to identify three main categories of business that made up the market in each segment. One

Figure 14.1: Scale and Growth Across Four Target Markets

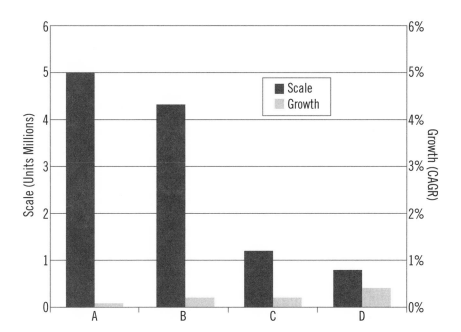

portion was greenfield projects: basically, new facilities being constructed. A second portion covered the replacement of older facilities that were no longer economical to operate. The final portion of the available market in each segment involved plant expansions. This firm felt that it could compete and win for greenfield projects and replacement projects, but that it had essentially no chance of winning expansion projects. It was almost certain that the incumbent supplier would be selected for the expansion, as the customer would wish to avoid significant duplicative costs that it would incur if there were two different suppliers' systems operating within a single facility.

Figure 14.2 shows the mix of business across these three categories, in each of the four markets.

From this perspective, with the three bars on the columns reflecting potential opportunities for our client, all four markets emerge as having some potential. The mix between greenfield and replacement projects, however, differs considerably between Markets A and B, where replacement projects dominate, and Markets C and D, where greenfield projects are the most plentiful.

This example illustrates our third recommendation to firms trying

Figure 14.2: Business Mix Across Markets

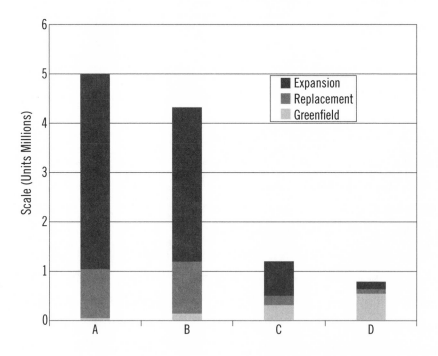

to identify their growth markets. In addition to thinking about opportunities to grow with existing customers—and in addition to paying attention to the growth segment of each market, it is important to consider the "Fit" between your firm and the prospect markets under consideration. For our client, there was no Fit whatsoever in the portions of each market associated with expansions. By contrast, for the incumbent suppliers in those markets, the Fit was superb for expansion projects. The only cases with any potential of a good Fit for our client were in the portions of each market associated with greenfield projects and replacement projects.

One final aspect of this case study deserves mention. When we did research with the customers in each of these four markets, we learned that their purchase decision drivers differed significantly. In Markets C and D, customers described almost a "Build it and they will come" environment, where demand was so great that new facilities would sell out almost as fast as they came on line. The most important factor in these customers' purchase decisions was the speed at which each competing supplier could bring a new facility into production. This happened to be a major strength of our client: Its technology facilitated installation and commissioning. On the other hand, for the replacement projects in Markets A and B, we heard decision makers focus on the project costs as the deciding factor; the bidding processes were designed to extract the last cent from bids, with the award going to the firm that came in at the lowest project cost. Our firm was not likely to fit this bill, as its competitors had consistently underbid it even in its currently served markets. So in this instance, the best Fit for our client was clearly the greenfield opportunities in Markets C and D.

Most market evaluations are not as straightforward as this case study. Still, along with the basic characteristics (scale, growth, profit potential) of the target markets under consideration, the concept of Fit is important to consider. In general, we focus on three dimensions of Fit in a market evaluation.[17]

The first of these dimensions is *purchase decision drivers*. Do they mesh with the strengths that are typically associated with wins for your firm? Is the market under consideration one in which price is the driving factor in purchase decisions? Or is buying behavior more heavily weighted toward product attributes, services, or other non-price factors? In the example above, the purchase decisions during replacement projects in markets A and B were driven by price, while those related to the greenfield projects in markets C and D were driven by product and service competencies such as speed to completion. Knowing what factors drive purchase decisions—and the degree to which the firm in question matches up with these key factors—is the first and typically the most important ingredient to an assessment of Fit. In the example above, the good match involved the greenfield projects, where the firm was in a strong position to create value for its customers and capture value for its own share-holders. Clearly there is no right answer in terms of purchase decision drivers, other than the extent to which they match well with your firm's competitive advantages.

The second dimension involves the firm's *starting point*. Do existing relationships or other factors provide a foundation for success? The example above was an exceptional case because there were sharp

17. See George F. Brown, Jr., and Atlee Valentine Pope, *Finding New Pathways to Profitable Growth* (Evanston, IL: Blue Canyon Partners, Inc., 2006).

and overwhelming differences across the markets; the quality of the starting point for expansion projects, defined by whether a firm was the incumbent supplier, essentially defined the choice in a "Go versus No Go" decision. Rarely is the starting point a deciding factor, but often it is an important one. We've seen, for example, numerous firms that succeed in global markets by following existing customer relationships into new geographic markets.[18] In other instances, firms realize a head start into adjacent product markets as a result of their preferred supplier position for their traditional product lines. The starting point is particularly important in determining the likelihood of near-term success in newly targeted markets.

The third dimension we examine in trying to gauge the Fit between a company and prospective market segments involves *key business drivers*. In our experience, the ability of a firm to succeed in the long term depends on the characteristics of the market and/or customer as well as the competencies of the supplier. The business drivers that are relevant vary from one setting to the next, but often they are obvious in the context of a specific evaluation. In one project, we found sharp differences across candidate markets along such factors as openness to innovation, willingness to build a relationship with a supplier, and the importance of worker productivity. The firm doing the evaluation had learned that its best and most profitable relationships were ones characterized by innovation, strong supplier-customer relationships, and value contributions to productivity. Naturally, the future markets more likely to be fertile for this firm were those where the same business drivers were important. In another

---

18. See Atlee Valentine Pope, and, George F. Brown, Jr., "Three C's of Global Account Management: Customers, Competencies, and Competitive Advantage," *Velocity* (Summer 1999).

instance, one firm had enjoyed strong success by helping its customers respond to succeeding generations of environmental regulations. Whether environmental regulation was important in a future market was likely to be a factor determining whether this firm's contributions would be valued.

The focus on opportunities for new market growth in recent years has emphasized global markets, and for good reason. Country markets like China, Brazil, and India have enjoyed economy-wide growth rates that only a few specialized niche markets in the United States or Western Europe have realized. Countless research articles have defined the arguments in favor of a strategy of globalization.[19] Many of them argue the benefits to be gained from aggregation (being able to serve a larger community of customers, taking advantage of a fixed cost base, and spreading investments across markets) and/or arbitrage (exploiting an advantage gained in one market to achieve success in other markets).

We see numerous examples where these foundations have yielded success in global markets. Unfortunately, the number of examples in which global market initiatives have failed, such as the acquisition of the Chinese auto parts manufacturer discussed earlier, is equally large. The factors that led to that acquisition's failure involved sharply different customer chains, distinct purchase decision drivers, and fundamental differences in the underlying economics of the business. A careful assessment of the fundamentals developed in section I of this book are prerequisite to making good decisions about global market expansion and developing an effective Go-to-Market Strategy.

---

19. See, for example, Pankaj Ghemawat, "Globalization: The Strategy of Differences," *Harvard Business Review* (November 2003).

We began this book with a focus on customer chains. More often than not, the customer chains that are in place in developed markets are not likely to be found in emerging markets. Furthermore, those in place in any one country may be unique for reasons of accident, tradition, culture, regulation, or other factors. One of our clients saw the sharp growth in automotive sales in China, which is now the largest car manufacturer, and wondered if its leading position as a repair parts supplier in the United States would enable it to be successful in China. What this supplier found was that the Chinese market had undeveloped customer chains, with few distributors or service centers of the types that dominate the U.S. market. While China was attractive to this firm for sound reasons, the firm's Go-to-Market Strategy had to be developed quite differently from the one that had been successful in the United States, where these later-stage customer chain participants were established and strong.

Along with exploring customer chains, we started section I with a focus on the means by which a firm can create value for its customers; we spotlighted the three possible means toward that end: helping customers gain market share, helping customers realize premium prices, and helping customers take costs out and thereby improve profitability. A firm seeking growth customers must consider whether its idea of how to satisfy these value creators is appropriate to the targeted market. The repair parts supplier had gained a strong following in the U.S. markets because its parts were repair friendly, a characteristic emphasized in its advertising and brand messages. The implication of being repair friendly was that the technician's productivity would be higher if it used this firm's products instead of a competitor's. In a high-wage environment like the United States, such productivity gains are money in the bank. But in China, one prospect that we interviewed asked us, "But what would we do with the technicians if they weren't doing repairs?" With labor plentiful and employment essentially guaranteed, productivity gains in China may not be the value creator that they typically are in markets like the United States.

The third lesson for deciding which customers will help your firm create and capture value involves developing the Market Map, which defines the elements of strategy that are likely to yield success within various market segments. In a project for a technology company targeting a new country market, we found three distinct segments. Our client provided factory floor equipment used by manufacturers to automate their production. One of the customer chains that we identified in the target country involved global firms that were producing for export markets. A second involved global firms that were selling into the domestic market in question. The third involved local firms also serving local end customers. The purchase decision drivers for these three customer chains are depicted in figure 14.3.

Only for the segment involving the export market was there a strong focus on technology and product attributes; the companies involved in these customer chains had to respond to the expectations and regulations of the export markets into which they sold. While there were some differences in the other two customer chain structures, in both cases, price was a key driver of purchase decisions at all stages of the customer chain.

Our client's successes in its existing markets were with customer chains located in the lower left quadrant, and its ongoing investments in

Figure 14.3: Technology Company Market Map

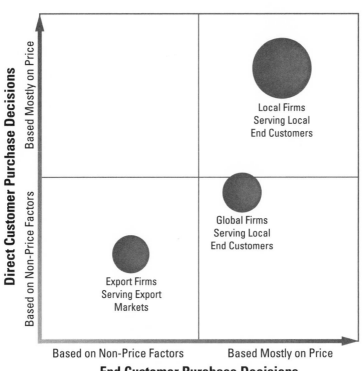

advancing its technology had generated a leadership position in those market segments. In the country under consideration, the segment that was similar represented only 16 percent of the overall market. Despite the overall size of the country market and its growth prospects, this firm's Fit was strong only in small segments and not in the segments where growth was taking place. As in the discussion of acquiring companies, as long as the customer chain is understood via the Market Map, it is not necessarily a bad idea to enter a market that requires a new approach to value creation. But it is always a bad idea to assume that a firm's existing approach to creating and capturing value will cross boundaries into new markets.

Overall, our advice to companies on the cusp of decisions about entering new global markets—or new markets defined by product vertical industry, or some other characteristic—is to reexamine the foundations of these decisions in terms of customer chains, the drivers of purchase decisions, the value lever opportunities, and the value capture options. In existing and new markets alike, the insights that emerge from exploring these foundations are central to success. The logic behind value creation for the markets in question must be fully understood. Only then can business leaders define the elements of a Go-to-Market Strategy that will win and yield rewards for shareholders.

Chapter 15

COLLABORATE WITH YOUR CHANNEL PARTNERS

Suppliers may be not only making decisions about entering new markets as part of a successful Go-to-Market Strategy, but also facing decisions about collaborating with channel partners.

During our conversation with one of our clients, a major manufacturer of high-technology equipment, one of his direct reports poked her head into the office and said, "Just a heads-up: I forwarded you a Voicemail 666 from [one of the firm's largest customers]." Picking up the quizzical look on our faces, he started to explain "Voicemail 666." He gave a recital of the content of a typical Voicemail 666 message: "You know how much we like working with your company, but we've gotten a proposal from Company X to supply your equipment at a pretty significant savings. We'd like to talk to you about an adjustment."

Our client went on to say that he heard that message so often, he found it easier to just code it as Voicemail 666 rather than go into the details every time. As we continued our discussion, he went into the reason behind this nickname:

We have basically three ways in which we go to market. First is our own direct sales force. That's how we started, and that's still our preferred strategy. We put a lot into this group. They're engineers. We do a lot of training, and they can bring a lot of value to our customers. The second group is the integrators and value-added resellers that are out there. We have to work with them, and some of them are really good in their niches. The best of the lot know an industry or an application, and can do magic in that arena. So we sell to them and let them repackage our products into their own systems. The third group involves the distributors and wholesalers, basically our industry's version of the big-boxes that serve consumer markets with a wide assortment of products at aggressive price points. They carry our products as well as everyone else's. If there is a demand, they're in the market.

Now here's the issue: All three groups are constantly getting into each other's turf. The integrators go to our direct sales force customers and tell them what they can do. They tell them they are experienced with our product—and it's often true, since some of them used to work for us. Some of these integrators would practically give away the hardware to get the job, because they make all their money on their labor. And the distributors go after both us and the integrators, often making a price pitch. Our stuff can be a perfect loss leader for some of them. Or they try to capture the integrator with a convenience pitch and put themselves in between us and the integrator, taking their cut. They don't have the overhead we have in terms of the experienced sales team. In fact, we often get pulled into the situation to deal with issues that these distributors don't even understand.

So that's how we get Voicemail 666 messages. One of our sales forces decides to go into competition with one of the others, and the end result is that we get a call about the pricing issue. It's a constant conundrum.

We explained to this client that his situation was hardly unique in the business-to-business world. It was, in fact, almost the textbook definition of the channel conflict that accompanies complex, competitive customer chains. In our own experiences, we've seen analogous situations in all sorts of industries: electrical equipment, fasteners, tools, packaging, medical equipment, telecommunications gear, you name it. Our guess is that managers from the business-to-business environment could give dozens and dozens of personal examples of this type of conflict.

MULTIPLE CHANNELS TO MARKET

The basis for the conflict becomes clear when looking at the complex customer chain structure described by our client, pictured in figure 15.1.

Add the normal real-world dynamics—multiple products, competitors at every stage of the chain, distinct end customer segments, discrete applications, and varied geography—and the already confusing picture becomes even more complex.

Figure 15.1: Complex Customer Chain

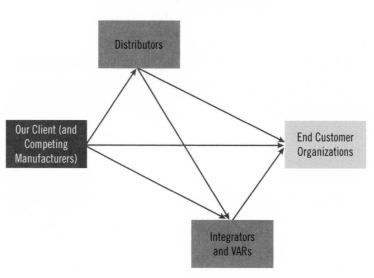

Even in this relatively simple customer chain structure, there are four distinct paths between our client (the supplier) and the end customer organizations, the final users of its products:

- Supplier ➜ End Customer

- Supplier ➜ Distributor ➜ End Customer

- Supplier ➜ Distributor ➜ Integrator ➜ End Customer

- Supplier ➜ Integrator ➜ End Customer

Each participant operating within such a structure will inevitably look forward into the customer chain and spot a prospect it would like to convert into a customer. Is the choice, then, between an eternity of Voicemail 666 messages or a decision to become another GEICO and eliminate the middleman?

We think not. In fact, the "eliminate the middleman" option is rarely practical. While a supplier can cut out the firm carrying its own products, it can't keep such firms from carrying competitors' products. And if there's one thing worse than a Voicemail 666 message, it's a voicemail message announcing that a customer has already switched to a competitor's product. So to some extent, receiving Voicemail 666 is a fact of life in the business-to-business arena.

Even more important, customer chain structures like those in this case study have emerged for a very good reason: The participants along them are all in some way creating value for their customers and working to capture it for their shareholders. This poses a very important opportunity (and challenge) for a leading firm: orchestrate your customer chains so there is a solid and reinforcing pattern of value creation contributions—and minimum conflict—among the firms involved.

Customer chains like those for this high-tech equipment manufacturer are prevalent in many business markets. Consider building systems suppliers (i.e., electrical, HVAC, plumbing) that sell through distributors and through contractors who install these products in homes and commercial buildings. Or vehicle aftermarket repair parts suppliers that sell through both wholesalers and retailers to automotive technicians who then do the actual installation on behalf of the consumers. In many of these customer chains, the manufacturer faces a sequence of intermediary channel partners between it and the final customer.

IDENTIFYING THE RIGHT SALES MODELS

Our approach to managing value creation in these types of complex customer chains is logical and constructive. It builds from an examination of the service contributions that are involved along the customer chain. When examining the services provided by various types of sales channel partners, we've found that customers place value on three distinct categories of services:

1. *Product-specific services* are closely associated with the physical product manufactured by the supplier in question. These often involve design, customization for a customer's particular application, engineering modifications, testing, quality assurance, training in the use of the product, support related to upgrades and successive generations of technology, and other services unique to a particular product technology, product application, or business environment.

2. *Systems-related services* help integrate a family of products into a functioning system that delivers performance in accordance with certain goals and requirements. These services typically fall within one of two categories:

   - Technical integration and linkage among individual products. These types of services ensure that components work seamlessly together, delivering superior performance and/or economics.
   - Project management challenges. These services encompass metrics related to system performance, on-time schedule, installation, commissioning, and budget.

- A key distinction of systems-related services is that they typically involve a spectrum of products from different manufacturers, and the key to success involves linkages across these products, rather than specific products in isolation.

3. *Distribution-related services* typically emphasize logistics and support to the eventual user of the product. Among the services in this category are order and fulfillment management, availability of a broad product line (to allow low-cost purchasing), record keeping, inventory and expediting (to ensure product availability and convenience for the buyer), finance and billing, returns and disposal, and other user support. More often than not, these types of services again span multiple products from multiple manufacturers.

It is hardly surprising that these three categories of services match up to the three types of participants on the customer chains described above—supplier, integrator, and distributor. In fact the latter two categories of services, in essence, define the value proposition of integrators and distributors. Understanding these various service categories, and who along the customer chain is most proficient in providing them, empowers a business-to-business firm to sort out the conundrum created by the multiple pathways to the end customer.

Consider the three-dimensional figure 15.2—the three categories of services described above serve as its three axes. Each axis reflects a category's level of importance to the end customer, from limited importance to significant importance. The various cubes within this larger cube represent different combinations of the three categories. The lower corner of the larger cube, shown in bold lines, provides a

Figure 15.2: Service Cube

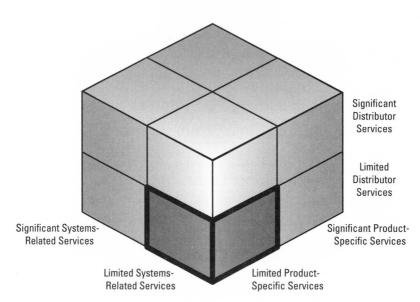

Significant
Distributor
Services

Limited
Distributor
Services

Significant Systems-
Related Services

Significant Product-
Specific Services

Limited Systems-
Related Services

Limited Product-
Specific Services

starting point for the analysis. Here, all three service categories hold only limited importance for the end customer.

This lower corner of the cube is a relatively rare situation—no surrounding services are particularly valued by the end customer. This is a signal that the end customers in this environment probably are price buyers. It would therefore be logical for the supplier to select the most efficient pathway for getting its products to the end customers.

Figure 15.3 summarizes the other seven possible cubes within this larger cube, the combinations that express how much the end customer might value the services delivered through various customer chain pathways.

These examples span multiple business environments—from health care to telecommunications to food and beverages to office

Figure 15.3: End Customer Evaluations of Services

	Product-Specific Services	Systems-Related Sevices	Distribution-Related Sevices	Description	Example
1	Limited	Limited	Limited		
2	Significant	Limited	Limited	Customer seeks supplier's technical design, engineering, and other product-related support.	Engine control module in a vehicle
3	Limited	Significant	Limited	Project involves seamless, on-time management to avoid delays and remain within budget.	Cables used in the build-out of a network for a financial institution
4	Limited	Limited	Significant	Customer's operations need to be up and running immediately.	Repair and replacement service and parts
5	Significant	Limited	Significant	Supplier tests and commissions initial equipment, and purchases the consumables that interact with the equipment on a regular basis.	Diagnostic equipment used in hospital laboratories, with consumables required for each individual test

	Product-Specific Services	Systems-Related Sevices	Distribution-Related Sevices	Description	Example
6	Significant	Significant	Limited	Several suppliers customize their equipment and/or software, with one party integrating the system.	Uninterruptible power supply incorporated into the critical power system, designed for a data center
7	Limited	Significant	Significant	Customer requires ongoing technical integration and installation of products in high-replacement environments.	Photoelectric sensors used in food production equipment
8	Significant	Significant	Significant	Customer seeks technology upgrades, integration, and reliable, sequenced delivery.	Controllers used in standardized robotic tools employed across multiple plant locations

products—in order to illustrate that these service combinations are commonplace across vertical markets and product lines.

What such diverse examples disguise, though, is that a single manufacturer is likely to operate in many, or sometimes all, of these business environments. The client from the beginning of this chapter, for instance, had a significant level of activity within each and every one of these service combinations. This equipment manufacturer's product line included some extraordinary technology offerings that were critical to certain high-value applications. The firm also manufactured some basic, simple products that were undifferentiated from those made by other participants in the industry. Some of its products were used in assembly-line operations as ingredients within other manufacturers' equipment; others were used in special engineered-to-order applications. Some of these products had long service lives and required replacement as a result of wear or damage.

These examples relate back to our core focus: identifying the opportunities for value creation and translating successes into value captured for shareholders. In the case of customer chains like those of our client, each participant along the customer chain has done exactly that in order to achieve success in some particular market segments. But in these complex cases, the manufacturer must acknowledge and accept another strategic reality: These value creation opportunities are likely to involve skills and competencies other than those harbored in its own organization. Channel partners, such as the integrators and distributors in this example, are in some segments as important to value creation as is the product manufacturer itself.

For our client, therefore, a key challenge—and a key step on the route toward lessening the frequency of Voicemail 666 messages—was to understand how the overall business was divided among these various service combinations. Our client had to develop insights for successfully managing the customer chains that required these different service combinations.

A number of frequent challenges come with these seven combinations of service contributions. Each has implications for value creation and capture, and each offers lessons on how to manage customer chains that involve intermediary channel partner relationships. These challenges are:

- Choosing the appropriate sales models and customer chain partners
- Supplying both the original product and the aftermarket service part
- Manufacturing the equipment and the associated consumables
- Building and sustaining a seat at the decision table

We've identified three primary sales models[20] that business-to-business suppliers can use in their Go-to-Market Strategy: a Supplier Direct model that does not involve any channel partner intermediaries; a Supplier Driven model that involves distributors or other channel intermediaries, within which the supplier takes the lead role in end customer relationships; and a Channel Driven business model that involves distributors or other channel intermediaries, within which the channel partner takes the lead role in end customer relationships.

Choices across these three business models can be defined by considering the service dimensions discussed above, as depicted in figure 15.4, where the supplier's own service contributions are reflected on

---

20. Atlee Valentine Pope and George F. Brown, Jr., *"Supplier Driven" and "Channel Driven" Business Models* (Evanston, IL: Blue Canyon Partners, Inc., 2006).

Figure 15.4: Sales Models and Services

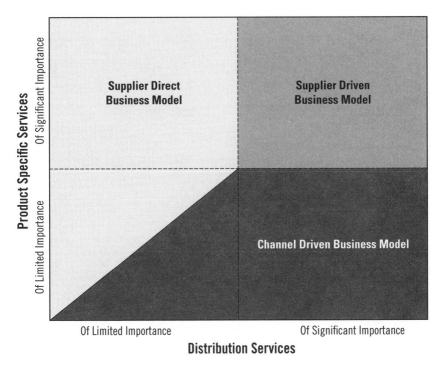

the vertical axis and those of its channel partner(s) are reflected on the horizontal axis.

Depending on which services are important to end customers, the appropriate business model varies. Supplier Direct relationships, for example, are most likely to be successful only when services from the supplier are critical to the other participants along the customer chain. In this example, in service combinations 2, 3, and 6 of figure 15.3, the supplier interacts directly with the integrator, value-added reseller, or contractor (and sees these participants as the customer in the latter two cases). A Supplier Driven business model, involving distributor partners, is most appropriate when service contributions from both the manufacturer and the channel partner are critical to end customers. Here, in combinations 5 and 8, where the supplier's technical know-how is of paramount importance (as are the distributor's expediting competencies), this approach is preferred. A Channel Driven business model, involving distributors in the lead sales and relationship roles, is suitable when only services from the channel partner are highly valued. Here, in combinations 4 and 7, where prompt delivery and dependable product availability are critical, this sales model is most appropriate.

These guidelines work for most firms. They sort out the labyrinth of customer chain segments and identify which ones fall into each of the seven combinations. Firms must select the appropriate business model and implement it through decisions about authorizations, bundling, and pricing. This can effectively guide the customer chain participants and reward them for providing the services that are valued by end customers. The idea is that matching the right services to your end customers will eventually mean opportunities for the manufacturers and channel partners to create and capture value. The guidelines emphasize that there is no "better" or "preferred" option. Rather, the choice depends on which service contributions are most likely to benefit customers further along the customer chain.

The service combination in which product-related services are the only services of significant value and the combination in which distributor-related services are the only services of significant value are frequently found in the OEM and service parts business markets. The OEM environment involves ingredients or modules supplied to an original equipment manufacturer—a carmaker, a computer manufacturer, an appliance manufacturer, a machine tool builder, or a manufacturer of some other type. These OEMs typically value the types of services that can best be provided by the supplier itself, as they are often looking for next-generation product improvements, solutions that involve the specific application of the supplier's product in their equipment, or other contributions. On the other hand, markets for repair and replacement parts, with availability of the parts in a timely and convenient manner being the service of most importance to end customers, place emphasis on the services of channel partners. We can map these tendencies in a similar fashion to our Market Map process. The two environments into which essentially the same part would

Figure 15.5: Service Decision Matrix

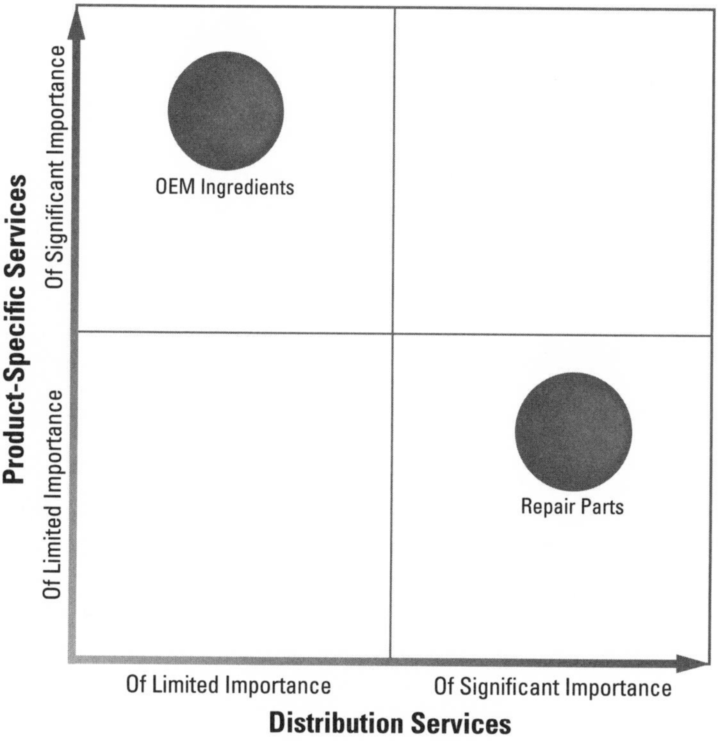

Product-Specific Services
Of Significant Importance
OEM Ingredients
Of Limited Importance
Repair Parts
Of Limited Importance   Of Significant Importance
Distribution Services

be sold are thus on quite different points of the diagram, as shown in figure 15.5.

The supplier in this market must manage two very distinct types of service delivery. In the OEM environment, the services required are closely associated with the product and its use. Such services are typically best provided through direct relationships with the end customers involved. In the repair parts environment, on the other hand, the service of most importance is timely product availability. This service is typically best performed by distributor organizations. The supplier must therefore develop and manage two distinct customer chain segments and ensure that its key decisions (e.g., direct technical support, distributor authorizations) are focused explicitly on the appropriate service environment for each segment.

A different situation exists when the supplier offers a combination of equipment and the consumables that are used during those equipment processes. Along with the hospital example in section 5 of figure 15.3, we've observed this situation with packaging equipment, test equipment, and fastener tools. The service valuation is depicted in figure 15.6.

If the end customer is to realize value from the supplier's offering, the supplier must provide both product-related services and distribution-related services. This requires supplier involvement and distributor contributions. The two organizations must work together effectively, be clear about each organization's roles and responsibilities, and coordinate their efforts as partners, not as competitors.[21] Most important,

---

21. Atlee Valentine Pope and George F. Brown, Jr., "Realizing Shared Successes in Co-destiny Relationships," *Velocity* (Second Quarter 2004).

Figure 15.6: Service Decision Matrix 2

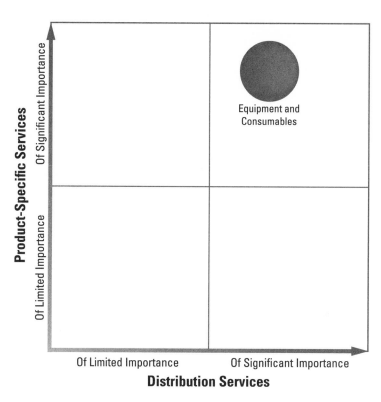

the supplier-distributor relationship must be managed to ensure collaboration rather than competitiveness.

The two preceding examples are clear when considered one at a time. But what happens when both situations coexist in a tangle of intertwined customer chains? All of a sudden, the logic—a Supplier Direct relationship for OEM parts, a Supplier Driven strategy for equipment and consumables, and a Channel Driven strategy for repair parts—can become confused. Two organizations working together could start to think of "the business" rather than "a mix of businesses." It is a constant challenge to ensure that all parties remain clear about the individual businesses; which business and relationship models are designed for each situation must not be confused in the mixing bowl of complex business-to-business relationships.

One of the largest business units in our high-tech OEM client's organization participated in at least six major market segments. Through interviews with the customer organizations involved, we developed a scoring system for the relative importance of

Figure 15.7: Service Decision Matrix 3

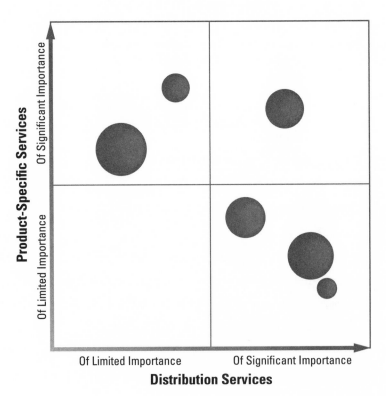

product-specific services and distribution-related services within each segment. Figure 15.7 shows the results of this analysis.

In this example, the customer segments harbored opinions across the spectrum with respect to both groups of services. Remarkably, the pathways into the market were poorly aligned with this assessment. Direct sales were the norm in four of the segments, including one in which product-specific services were viewed with limited importance while distribution-related services were viewed as very important. Yet note the bubble at the far left of the figure: Distributors were authorized to sell this product line to end customers that placed little value on distributor services and that signaled the critical importance of product-specific services. Other inconsistencies were plentiful. Those outcomes were the natural result of "least common denominator" and "one size fits all" rules that can entangle participants in complex customer chains. Our client had to begin a journey of sorting out the complexities by focusing on the service requirements of each individual business segment.

As our clients proactively manage their complex customer chains, seeking to match their service delivery efforts to end customer valuation, many have realized the need for a "seat at the table" with its end customers. This is particularly true in the market segments in which product-specific services are critical to success. Some of these environments were managed through Supplier Direct business models, and others through Supplier Driven models. In each case, the supplier took action to earn itself a seat at the table by delivering high-value surrounding services.

To maintain an intimate relationship with end customers, firms often have to reevaluate their long-standing approach toward major customer management, as we've discussed in previous chapters. Many organizations define their strategy according to the needs of accounts that meet a certain size or scale of activity. But firms that rethink their customer chains, taking into account the factors that are critical to success with their various customers, often find it useful to redefine the basis for viewing a relationship as strategic. According to this new definition, a relationship is strategic if success depends upon the delivery of high-value, product-specific services.

Another change that firms often make is in their perspective on third-party participants in their customer chains. The internal mind-set of our high-tech OEM client was that these third parties were, at best, a necessary evil; at worst, they were the very reason for the hated Voicemail 666 message stream. This client revised its perspective, acknowledging the competency of these channel partners in providing certain value-creating services critical to end customers. The firm began to deliberately choose integrators and distributors on the basis of their service delivery competencies, designating them as valued partners and incorporating them into its family.

This sea change in thinking is expressed by a visual used in one of the firm's new pieces of literature. The visual looked something like figure 15.8, with our client identified as Company XYZ.

What this organization communicated clearly through this graphic was its awareness of the multiplicity of services that were important to its customers. Some of these services—core services associated with its products, those it deemed necessary to earn key seats at the table with its customers—it could provide directly. But this firm's messages also emphasized other services valued by customers, communicating loud and clear that it had invested in best-in-class, third-party relationships to supply those services.

Figure 15.8: Key Service Providers in Customer Chain Map

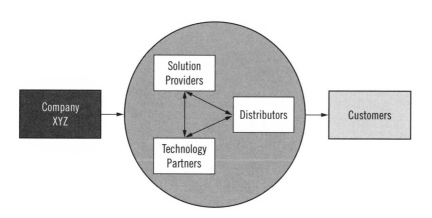

Along with its change in mind-set and in customer communications, the firm took steps away from the status quo and toward a future in which these co-destiny relationships were part of a deliberately developed structure rather than a historical accident. In truth, some of this organization's relationships weren't constructive but were in fact more the product of an overzealous salesperson than a good business decision. The firm went through its service categories "cube," cell by cell, and identified the customer chain participants involved in each cell. It rated their contributions using a scorecard based on which service competencies were important to value creation within that cell of the cube. It terminated a few third-party channel partnerships, either by not renewing agreements or by setting more appropriate requirements; those that couldn't (or wouldn't) meet them opted out of that portion of the business altogether. The firm also established criteria for entering new relationships based on the same scorecards.

Our Voicemail 666 client eventually categorized its business into the eight cells of the cube, and it used this visual as a means of understanding the customer chains and service competencies that were the key to success in each of the combinations. The firm also used this visual to quickly identify Voicemail 666 situations that came when it strayed outside of the appropriate cell. It began to focus on service contributions as an essential tool through which it managed its sales models, channel partner relationships, reward structures, and business plans.

This firm implemented a number of creative approaches in order to do a better job of segmenting its market and matching its decisions to the individual segments. One action involved unbundling certain technical support services from the products themselves. This way, product prices in applications that did not require technical support would not be undercut by intermediaries that took advantage by offering discounts. This unbundled pricing strategy helped the firm capture additional revenues from customers who did require such technical services.

A second change was even more significant. Previously, this firm had basically opened its catalog to distributors and integrators when it accepted them as authorized channel partners, offering them a discount pricing structure. In calculating the discounts, the most important variable in the equation was the total volume of purchases from the firm. When the firm analyzed its business in each of the eight cube cells, however, it found significant distinctions across its product line from one cell to the next. For example, certain products—which in truth were more like platforms allowing customer-specific customization—appeared exclusively in the four cells where product-related services were very important. Meanwhile, other products were almost always in the four cells where product-related services were of little to no importance. The firm changed its channel authorization policies so they covered only the products in the latter category, and it restructured its distributor pricing scheme to reward sales volume only in the four cells where valuation of product-related services was low.

These actions reduced the frequency of Voicemail 666 messages, but more important, they eliminated the misalignments that were open to exploitation by the two groups of intermediaries.

Many organizations involved in business-to-business customer chains find themselves sewn into a patchwork quilt of pathways into the multiple markets they serve. Such complex customer chains are natural—the product of their distinct business environment, a succession of historical decisions, or responses to overtures or competitive challenges that occurred from time to time. One outgrowth of this type of development is that the various pathways frequently become confused; they often begin to compete with one another and finally lead to unintended outcomes, such as dreaded Voicemail 666 messages.

Complex customer chains can be unraveled, however, when a firm's focus is on its end customers' service requirements and how to create and capture value with those needs in mind. These service requirements typically span three distinct types of services, and it is possible to organize a firm's business into combinations defined by the types that are valued by each end customer segment. Based on that categorization, a firm can make decisions about which channel partner relationships should be used to reach each segment. By defining which third-party relationships will be critical to success, firms can determine the roles and responsibilities—the perspectives and actions that will create and capture value—that should be assigned to each partner as part of an overall Go-to-Market Strategy.

Chapter 16

BRING YOUR SUPPLIERS INTO THE VALUE CREATION PROCESS

Making decisions about the intermediary organizations that operate on some customer chains between a manufacturer and the end customers—distributors, dealers, contractors, and integrators—is often central to a firm's overall Go-to-Market Strategy. We argued in the previous chapter that many end customers place considerable value on the specific services offered by such organizations, which have themselves built systems and competencies to ensure their ability to deliver such value. The firms that consider these intermediaries to be important co-destiny partners in value creation are the ones most likely to be successful. In this chapter, we examine a second group of customer chain participants that frequently must also be considered partners in value creation and rewarded with a share of that value: the suppliers of components, capital equipment, and services that enable a firm to operate.

Over the past decade, most businesses have paid close attention to managing their supplier base. Such investments have yielded considerable value to these firms' shareholders. Supply base initiatives have helped these firms achieve an improved cost position and facilitated their transition into global markets. In many situations, such firms define their supply base as a source of competitive advantage, with that phrase often truly meaning cost advantage. We believe that firms can realize even greater levels of success with certain suppliers whose contributions can be of strategic value. Our research has uncovered ways to encourage best-in-class customer behaviors focused on a carefully selected group of suppliers. When firms implement such programs, these suppliers can contribute successfully to value creation, and both participants will reap the benefits.

Remember the company leader in chapter 1 who lamented that his firm's customers "treat us like a commodity"? In working with leading business-to-business suppliers across diverse industries, we frequently encounter firms that complain about their customers not recognizing the value that they provide. Firmwide initiatives to strengthen contributions—whether through product development, services, brand initiatives, or other approaches—are consistently included as high-priority elements of these organizations' annual plans. Much of our own research has focused on how business-to-business suppliers can become vital to their customers, and we've learned how both strategy and relationship management fit into that equation. We've shared many of these lessons in the previous chapters of this book.

Yet discussions in which we hear the message "Our suppliers aren't contributing at the level we need" are rare, except when the shortfall is in either price or delivery. This is both surprising and disappointing. Organizations that aren't looking to expand their relationships and demand more of their suppliers are missing out on opportunities for greater value creation and capture. Over the course of numerous consulting projects and research initiatives, we've interviewed literally thousands of business leaders and learned about their perspectives on suppliers and their contributions. In fewer than a dozen instances did an interviewee say that he or she was unable to provide an example of a supplier success story. Most interviewees have numerous ones from which to choose, and the vast majority of those success stories have nothing to do with price, delivery, or other such metrics.

Rather, the success stories typically focus on other types of contributions, often unexpected ones, brought to them by their suppliers. Sometimes the success story involves a new product or technology advancement. Sometimes it involves a way of taking costs out of the combined supplier-customer systems. Sometimes it involves an insight about how the two firms in combination can become more successful with the customers further along on the customer chain. Sometimes it involves an idea about how the relationship can be transported into some new market environment. Sometimes it involves creative ideas about how shifts in the roles and boundaries of the two firms can result in better performance. The examples are almost as diverse as the business environments from which these supplier success stories originate. All of them had the characteristic, from the perspective of the customer telling the story, of the supplier creating value for their organization. We think that there is great value in turning the telescope in the other direction, with the obvious question being "How can we as a customer motivate the best suppliers to bring their best value contributions to us?"

FOUNDATIONS FOR SUCCESS

A client in the medical equipment industry held a workshop to examine its history with suppliers from many different segments of its business. As part of that process, teams developed case studies of various supplier relationships, focusing particularly on ones that had yielded some meaningful contributions. As the group analyzed these case studies, it found many characteristics that were unique to a particular relationship or technology. But several elements were common to all the success stories, and these provided a starting point for developing a blueprint for success with suppliers.

First among the common elements was a sense of long-term alignment between the supplier and this firm. In one case, the executive responsible for the relationship observed, "It has been clear to both of our organizations that we're in this together for the long run." Another executive commented, "We saw positive reasons for this relationship—ones that were based on [the supplier's] particular focus and competency, as opposed to looking at them as a temporary fix to a problem or as a relationship we were forced into because of our cost structure."

Interviews with suppliers also confirm the importance of long-term alignment of interests. One supplier we interviewed commented on the reasons for this:

> There are at least three reasons why a longer-term perspective is critical to our success. First is the fact that it takes a while to build knowledge and familiarity. Without that, we're shooting in the dark, and it's hard to hit the bull's-eye [that way]. Second is the fact that we need to create a sense of confidence on the part of our customer. No one is going to go out on a limb until there is some history on which to rely. The third reason is that

we aren't going to invest our best efforts and best ideas in a transient relationship. There's just no payoff from doing that.

We hear similar thoughts over and over from suppliers. Just as the customer is looking for a commitment from them, they are looking for a commitment from their customers. When there is sufficient alignment between the two organizations to sustain a long-term relationship, the relationship can lead to supplier success stories.

The second common element of the case studies developed during this workshop was effective communications channels between the two organizations. One participant commented that successful collaborations had a "What-Who-When" dimension: The two firms knew What to talk about, Who should be engaged in the discussions, and When the discussions needed to take place. When any of the three weren't in place, the communications were likely to be ineffective.

The case study examples compiled during our client's workshop provided insights along all three dimensions. With respect to What, there was one very frequent element: Discussions between the supplier and its customer frequently were focused on their external environment, rather than being limited to discussions about the interactions between them. This focus is unusual; we often hear supplier complaints about the ways their customers insulate them from the broader business environment in which they operate. "We'll tell you what you need to know" is the message that suppliers typically hear from their customers. Some even report a second element to the communication: "And we don't want you mucking around in our markets and with our customers, trying to get around us."

The Who dimension of supplier-customer communication involves two themes. First, there are champions of the relationship within both organizations—individuals who take a proactive role in making sure that appropriate interactions take place, that information is shared, and that the organizations are working together effectively. Second, communications are not restricted to these point persons, but instead involve numerous touch points across business functions, up and down the organization, and in the various regions where collaboration takes place.

Many of these latter interactions take place independently of any specific request by the champions; however, they may be a direct result of efforts that the relationship champions have made over the years to foster familiarity and comfortable working relationships among the appropriate experts and business leaders. One individual participating in our client's workshop, a relationship champion for her company, noted that many of the best supplier contributions originated from some unexpected interaction between individuals, as opposed to taking place in the context of formal, planned interaction.

The When dimension of the equation focuses on the future. A key lesson is that discussions need to take place in a timely fashion so the two organizations can react and respond to opportunities and issues. As such, interactions must occur between the two organizations at a high-frequency cadence. One case study developed during the workshop involved a business relationship between two participants that had an annual meeting, during which there were frequent laments about opportunities that had passed. Both organizations expressed regret over new product and technology initiatives that had failed to yield value because their plans were not in sync. The case studies that involved high-frequency interactions, on the other hand, did not share this characteristic; these organizations were more able to get action plans in place in a timely fashion and to coordinate their schedules for effective linkage.

Furthermore, supplier success stories rarely just happen. Rather, they need to be motivated and managed by an organization and individuals whose goal is to create an environment within which strong and positive contributions can be made. Strong relationships are essential to creating such an environment, as discussed in the first section of this book. The individuals at this workshop viewed maintaining supplier relationships as their job, and their organization had much earlier recognized that suppliers could play an important role in the company's success, in some cases filling a void that could not be effectively addressed using internal resources. These relationships were often long-standing ones, and the medical equipment firm worked with its partners to draw clear road maps for how the relationship would evolve into the future. Yet the group's motivation throughout the workshop was to see how they could take these relationships to an even higher level. This organization, in our experience, is atypical. We've encountered relatively few firms that have such a positive, multifaceted approach to supplier relationships.

One individual with whom we worked in another industry commented, "We've gotten very good at managing our supply chain in the bidding process, with some real payoff in terms of achieving cost savings and finding new, low-cost sources of supply." But he went on to note, "We have no parallel track record of success in developing high-value supply relationships—ones that yield contributions in terms of how we're positioned in our markets or how much value we deliver to our customers through new innovations and new technologies." Still another firm, one that was attempting to create a strategic supplier program, heard this message from one of its suppliers: "If we'd shown you new innovations and product extensions, you'd have written a request for proposals and put our ideas up for bid."[22]

These situations are the far more common ones. Supplier relationships are most often managed reactively: The organization defines a need, puts out some form of a request for proposals, and selects the lowest-cost offer from among the firms that can meet the company's specifications. This type of process is designed to generate participation among competing suppliers; efforts are frequently made to simplify the requirements, thus allowing more and more firms to bid, and driving bids to the lowest possible level. E-auctions are one example of such a process. The suppliers and customers with whom we've spoken mostly agree that this approach makes it hard for a firm to showcase and get credit for innovation, services, or new solutions to their customer's problem.

Clearly, there is great inconsistency between these typical approaches to supplier relationships and the esteem the companies profess to hold for the suppliers. This suggests the need for a different approach, one that encourages suppliers to bring their best contributions—and not just lower cost—to their customers. Our research reveals the steps that firms can take to develop a Relationship Advantage with their suppliers as part of an effective Go-to-Market Strategy that will result in supplier contributions to the value creation process and shareholder rewards.

---

22. Atlee Valentine Pope and George F. Brown, Jr., *Best-in-Class Behaviors in Business-to-Business Relationships* (Evanston, IL: Blue Canyon Partners, Inc., 2007).

MESSAGES FROM THE MARKET

Among our interviews have been several thousand pairs of organizations in business relationships, across diverse vertical industries. The suppliers in these relationships provided a wide variety of ingredients, capital equipment, infrastructure, and services; their offerings ranged from highly differentiated, patented products to the most basic of commodities. The customers in these relationships not only spanned numerous industries, but also crossed global markets and ranged from industry leaders to new entrants into their markets. The products and services offered by these customer organizations also covered the spectrum in terms of the level of differentiation they enjoyed. Both suppliers and customers ranged from Fortune 100 firms to small businesses, although a significant majority were larger firms. Typically our interviewees came from multiple job functions within an organization, so we often heard the perspectives of individuals in purchasing, operations, sales, and general management.

In these interviews, we asked open-ended questions about supplier success stories, allowing the interviewee to provide his or her own definition of how a supplier contributed to success. The most important insights—those that provide actionable points—came as a result of follow-up questions about what enabled that success story to be written. Some interviewees had an immediate answer to this question; they had already attempted to understand the drivers of an important success for their firm and to translate such learning into their own processes and relationships. Other interviewees claimed that they had no idea about the origin of the success story. They just shrugged their shoulders and said, "It came out of nowhere."

We have learned that success stories don't have a single point of origin. Rather, multiple customer practices create an environment in which suppliers are able to make contributions that lead to success. Several dozen of these best customer practices have emerged from our research with frequency, providing valuable input on making business decisions about how to manage supply relationships. We believe that these practices should be implemented deliberately, with a focus on those suppliers whose contributions are of strategic importance to the firm from an internal perspective, a customer chain perspective, or both. Making the conscious decision to apply these relationship-building practices is an important part of any Go-to-Market Strategy.

Developing a Relationship Advantage with suppliers isn't an easy task. Firms must create a multidimensional environment within which supplier-customer relationships can flourish; the typical "Do A, then B happens" sequence leads to one-time-only outcomes. We also find that results take time. The vast majority of success stories involve ongoing relationships rather than relationships recently started from scratch. The very few examples of successfully developing brand-new relationships all involved a technology breakthrough, so in some sense these are more research and development success stories than supplier success stories.

Figure 16.1 describes the best-in-class customer practices for creating a Relationship Advantage with key suppliers. This table provides three examples of possible behaviors associated with each customer practice, ranging from behaviors that do not support the practice to those that support it in the best way possible.

We should point out the inherent conflict between following these "Best Behaviors" and encouraging open, aggressive competition between suppliers. For almost every item on the list, it is hard to conceive of

Figure 16.1: Customer Practices

Customer Practice	Unsupportive Behaviors	Supportive Behaviors	Best Behaviors
Information Flow	The information flows in one way and is limited to "need to know" messages.	Regular meetings take place to ensure effective communication.	Ensure solid, two-way information flow about all topics relevant to the success of the relationship.
Outcome Focus, Enabling Solutions	Interactions focus only on products, services, prices, etc.	The customer provides the supplier with insights about "what success means."	The firms share a clear under-standing of the outcomes— along multiple dimensions—that yield shared suc-cesses; the firms are open to new ways of achiev-ing success.
An Organiza-tional Ap-proach to the Relationship	The relationship is "purchasing to sales," mostly defined by the individuals involved.	Organization-wide understanding of the relationship is facilitated.	Responsibilities for the success of the relationship are shared across business functions and units in both organizations.
Openness of the Relationship, with Multiple Touch Points	The relationship is channeled through a single touch point.	Forums are created for interaction among subject matter experts.	Aggressive steps are taken to ensure connectivity between the two firms across job functions, geography, and topics.

Customer Practice	Unsupportive Behaviors	Supportive Behaviors	Best Behaviors
Margin Management	The firms battle for margin, with improvements expected to come out of the "pot" shared by the two organizations.	The firms recognize that each must be able to reward its shareholders, and they incorporate a long-term belief that the other's financial success is important to the relationship.	The firms focus on wins against their competitors and on opportunities to reach new growth markets, with relationships enabling both to share in the rewards from these external successes.
Systems Perspective with Respect to Processes and Linkages	Roles of and boundaries between the supplier and the customer are inviolate.	The supplier and the customer collaborate on process improvement in an open environment.	The supplier and the customer are open to changes in roles and boundaries in order to optimize performance.
Clarity of Performance Metrics	Customer messages are limited to problem situations.	Goals are clearly defined, and performance is jointly monitored and measured.	Collaboration around performance goals is a tool for sustaining the relationship.
Ability to Resolve Problems	Problems fester and result in finger-pointing.	The two firms find work-arounds that remove the problem from center stage.	The two firms identify and resolve the root causes of the problem.
Timely and High-intensity Interactions	Interactions are infrequent, typically occurring around problems or contracts.	Regular interactions take place, with a defined agenda and planned roster of participants.	Relationships between the customer and the supplier ensure informal as well as formal interactions.

Customer Practice	Unsupportive Behaviors	Supportive Behaviors	Best Behaviors
"Seat at the Table" Involvement in Planning and Problem Solving	Customer plans are made without involvement of the supplier.	The supplier is brought into discussions that draw upon its area of expertise.	The customer routinely involves the supplier in open-ended discussions of plans and problems.
Focus on the Future	Discussions focus on recent performance and problems.	The supplier is provided a road map defined by the customer's plans.	The customer and supplier collaborate on developing plans and priorities.
Focus on the Customer Chain	Suppliers have no visibility beyond their direct customer.	Customers provide suppliers with information about and access to subsequent-stage customers.	Suppliers and customers collaborate to understand subsequent-stage customers and their priorities.

implementing the Best Behaviors with multiple suppliers who are going to compete for contracts at various points in time. Not only would the customer be unlikely to involve multiple suppliers in the ways suggested above, but the suppliers themselves would be unlikely to respond if their head-to-head competitor were also involved in the interactions. We've heard far too often the supplier complaint cited earlier: "We brought them an idea, and next thing we knew, they'd put it into a request for proposals and sent it to our competitors."

IDENTIFYING STRATEGIC SUPPLIERS

A customer's first steps in developing a Relationship Advantage with suppliers must be to determine which supplier contributions are important for value creation and to create a framework for supply management. This process is necessary to identify those suppliers for which the Best Behavior practices are appropriate. Customers can often implement many or even most of the Supportive Behaviors widely across their supply base, even when competition remains a core element of the supply management framework. But going beyond that point to the Best Behaviors level should typically be reserved for supply relationships that are of strategic importance to the customer.

In fact, the success of these practices depends heavily on having the right supplier partners. It is important not only to identify which supplier contributions can be of strategic importance, but also to determine which supplier partners can potentially become truly strategic suppliers within a well-developed relationship.

We've helped our clients apply these concepts by creating a supplier scorecard that ranks candidate suppliers according to their potential for success if elevated into a strategic supplier position. While the scorecard varies from industry to industry, it typically includes three principal ingredients:

1. **An assessment of the supplier's commitment to the relationship.** Does this supplier view the relationship as an important one? Strategic relationships are two-sided coins; the supplier should view its customer as a strategic customer to the same extent that the customer views the supplier as a strategic supplier. The supplier must exhibit behaviors that provide evidence of this— investment in the relationship, a commitment to its success, outstanding understanding of the business environment, etc. Also, the context of the supplier's business (including its relationships with competitors) must be considered if the success of the relationship is likely to depend on confidentiality or "first-look" collaboration with respect to product and technology development.

2. **Proof of a successful track record.** Can this supplier be counted upon to deliver? The supplier must have a proven ability to meet the "on time, in full, at quality" standards relevant to the relationship, and this track record must extend to all dimensions of the relationship, not just shipments of product. What's more, the organization's foundations should be consistent with ongoing success. It should offer process capabilities relevant to the relationship, a situational awareness that allows it to be ahead of problems and opportunities, and even best-practice standing in areas critical to success in the relationship.

3. **Evidence of strength in the areas where strategic contributions to value creation are expected.** Does this supplier have

the potential to contribute further in the areas that motivated its possible elevation to strategic supplier status? To a certain extent, the first two ingredients resolve the concern that the choice might turn out to be a bad one; this third ingredient goes further, focusing on the potential for the supplier to become a future success story. Considerations include visibility of the supplier's contributions to customers further along the customer chain, the supplier's track record of innovation vis-à-vis its competitors, the supplier's breadth and potential to evolve in sync with the relationship, the supplier's geographic and industry footprint, and the level of intensity that the supplier brings to the relationship.

Clearly, a full evaluation is required before the selection of a supplier to be developed into a strategic partner.

MANAGING STRATEGIC SUPPLIER RELATIONSHIPS

Once the appropriate partner has been chosen, a firm must take the right steps to position its supplier relationship for success. Figure 16.1's summary of key customer practices is useful for providing a few examples. The first observations relate to information flow (see the table's first row). Practice shortfalls in this area, more than in any other area, are cited by suppliers as the cause of avoidable problems in their relationships with customers. We've heard the "If only we'd known . . ." lament so many times, accompanied by so many concrete examples, that we believe it to be true. When we've asked the customer about that same information gap, we've heard responses such as "I had no idea that they didn't know . . ." or "At the time, it didn't seem relevant . . ." Firms that successfully create a supportive supplier environment, on the other hand, have taken aggressive steps to put in place those foundations for sharing knowledge. A key to success in creating a positive supplier relationship is to have regular interactions, guided by a preplanned agenda. The stronger practitioners go beyond this; they systematically inventory the information needs of their suppliers—not just product specifications and order metrics, but insights related to plans, problems, forecasts, and other factors that might have an impact on the success of the relationship.

The second topic involves the desired outcome around which the relationship is centered. In the case of non-strategic suppliers, the outcome focus is often quite simple: The supplier is expected to deliver a certain quantity of product at certain specs on a certain date at a defined price. For strategic suppliers, the outcome focus can be far more complex: The supplier is expected to help solve a marketing challenge, resolve a technical issue, respond to a new regulation, identify ways to reduce system life-cycle costs, help leapfrog the competition in a new market, or make some other multidimensional contribution to the customer's success. Writing a request for proposal so specific that it does not allow for new, innovative solutions is the antithesis of an effective focus on strategic outcomes. Meanwhile, the best-practice customers engage their key suppliers in an open dialogue about where they are trying to go and when they are trying to get there. These organizations also ensure that they are ready to hear and consider suppliers' new ideas about how to facilitate such journeys.

The focus on an organizational approach to the relationship and on adequate touch points (the third and fourth rows of the table) reflects two key prerequisites to creativity: innovation and unexpected contributions. In significant supplier-customer relationships, it is not possible for any individual, no matter how skilled, on either side of the relationship to bring the full array of knowledge and expertise to the discussion. This is sometimes possible in transactional relationships, but the more that the outcome focus involves multiple dimensions, the more that organization-wide involvement is required. So while a strong procurement manager or account executive can keep transactional relationships on a positive keel, as the contributions become more elaborate and significant, it takes an organizational commitment to succeed. In best-practice companies, we've seen purchasing executives take the lead in assigning responsibilities to other departments as part of their formal goal structure. When it comes to the success of a supplier relationship, one company's mantra—"If it's in the performance goals, it matters, but if it's not, it doesn't"—is probably somewhat close to a universal truth. If a supplier relationship is important to the firm, it should identify entire business units willing to work toward that success. Strong relationship champions from the two organizations should formally discuss the question of touch points by asking, "Who will be important to our success over the next year?" They must then bring these individuals into contact with one another and ensure continuation of their interactions.

Margin management is a theme that has emerged over and over in our research. When we examined the challenges of channel conflict involving supplier-distributor relationships,[23] margin management scored highest among the themes that often get between the par-

---

23. Atlee Valentine Pope and George F. Brown, Jr., "Realizing Shared Successes in Co-destiny Relationships," *Velocity* (Second Quarter 2004).

ticipants in such relationships. In one set of interviews, as mentioned in chapter 1, interviewees from both the supplier and the distributor even characterized the other party as a "constant deterrent to a profit goal." Obviously, suppliers that have that perspective about its customer are less than likely to make meaningful contributions to its success, and customers that feel that way about their suppliers are unlikely to invite them into important plans and decisions.

At a minimum, for a supportive environment along this dimension, both organizations must feel that the relationship is consistent with their long-term business success; they must trust the other party to behave with integrity and reasonableness in negotiations and contract processes. In the thousands of interviews we've done, it has been revealing how few organizations, on either side of the relationship, have unrealistic expectations; neither expects the other organization either to be a pushover or to provide charity relief. At the same time, businesses are in business—they do not expect unbusinesslike outcomes. Usually these outcomes occur when a prospectively solid relationship is pushed beyond the limits of good business decisions. In this regard, firms that have solid information-sharing programs and effective touch points are far better than others at avoiding this outcome.

At the Best Behaviors end of the spectrum are the relatively few supplier-customer relationships that use formal planning to help the team win against competitor teams in its market, or that collaborate to reach new markets that are attractive in terms of scale, growth prospects, or margins. The few examples of such collaboration suggest that the rewards from such a focus are extraordinary. Working with one supplier-customer team that did about a half billion dollars of business in partnership, we completed a structured assessment of growth prospects, examining new vertical markets, new geographic markets, and opportunities for new product and systems development. The participants in this review operated without company hats, set shared priorities, and agreed upon three initiatives for implementation. Three years later, they had doubled their average annual growth rate and both firms were celebrating bottom-line results at record levels. Not every supplier-customer team has the same opportunities that were available to these firms. But partners that focus on their growth opportunities are well positioned to translate that focus into rewards that come from their markets—and out of the pockets of their competitors—rather than having to argue over the division of rewards between their own organizations.

Practices related to the systems perspective developed by the two organizations are based on a simple fact: There are more opportunities for optimization when the full system is considered than when two parts of the system are considered individually and in isolation. We emphasized this point in our earlier discussion about business systems and services and the potential of the Relationship Advantage for customers located in the lower right quadrant of the Market Map. This same potential exists looking backward into the supply chain.

Strong information networks and effective touch point relationships—some of the benefits of the best practices we described earlier—make it easier to get at these harder-to-find optimization opportunities. We've seen best-practice relationships tackle reverse audits and develop collaborative projects in an attempt to improve processes and pinpoint unnecessary costs. Our study of the automotive industry identified situations in which collaboration resulted in lower supplier prices—without affecting the margins of either firm.

But such successes often required changes in the roles of and boundaries between the two firms.[24] Openness to such changes is both an element of the philosophy that customers must accept in building strategic relationships with their partner suppliers and a statement of confidence in the relationship choices they've made. When an organization adopts the systems perspective, the potential for meaningful, cost-effective improvements is significant.

The reaction of some of our clients to the table's focus on clarity of performance measures (the seventh row) has been "Duh!"—and in fact, this is an obvious prelude to success in making contributions that matter. But these same clients are stunned by how many examples we can cite of relationships that failed because the two organizations simply were not on the same page. Perhaps the importance of clear performance metrics was a point best made by our customer whose organization fits well with the description of a best-in-class customer: "That's table stakes."

Problem solving is another customer practice that can be either a major negative or a major positive. We have yet to see a single supplier-customer relationship that didn't experience problems at some point in time. What distinguishes relationships is the ability to solve these problems. In the worst cases, the problems recur and even become the focal point of interactions. More supportive approaches involve collaboration to ensure that the problem doesn't interfere with the relationships. We've seen numerous examples of work-arounds that have achieved that outcome. For example, product shortages are often among the failures that threaten relationships; decisions to increase

---

24. Atlee Valentine Pope, Jon T. Gabrielsen, and George F. Brown, Jr., *Win the Day: Managing Price Pressures in the Automotive Industry* (Evanston, IL: Blue Canyon Partners, Inc., 2003).

safety stocks and review orders manually are among the means of keeping these problems under control. But we've also seen collaboration that got at the root causes of the problem and identified genuine solutions. In one instance, when the two firms focused on the underlying forecasting systems that were being used by the supplier to plan production and shipments, they found ways to strengthen these systems, resolving the problem without added cost or artificial overrides. This example is in the category of a Best Behaviors approach to problem solving.

Encouraging timely and high-intensity interactions (the ninth row of figure 16.1) is another practice that appears to be obvious to firms whose relationships have been successful. The messages that we've heard from such firms about this practice have focused on three keys to success. First, they suggest that "timing is everything"; essential contributions are as much about the right time as the right idea. Frequent and intense interactions are one way to ensure that discussions happen early enough to allow results at the right time. Second, we frequently hear that the two organizations put pressure on each other to "take it to a higher level"—in a constructive fashion, but one that nonetheless isn't particularly satisfied with the status quo. The cultures associated with such relationships are overwhelmingly performance oriented. One individual characterized its partner supplier's position as "the most stable one in our supply base," yet explained that its behavior was like that of "someone with a wolf pack closing in on them." That is a good characterization of intensity in the relationship. Third, these success stories emerge from unexpected directions and were triggered by informal interactions—one of the main reasons for building strong and diverse touch points between the supplier and the customer organizations.

Among the practices that we hear praised over and over in discussions of strong relationships is the customer allowing the supplier a seat at the table in appropriate forums and discussions. One customer organization that has been quite successful in creating a contributing supply team did a systematic review within its firm, asking the question "If that supplier were part of our company, what meetings would we have them attend?" As the meetings were identified, the firm asked the question "Why are we excluding them?" and often found that there was no good reason for doing so. An executive in this firm noted, "They are going to hear about our plans eventually, as one of our strategic suppliers. So why not bring them into the discussion early enough to contribute?" As the firm implemented that idea, it found that its suppliers had much to contribute and that they typically participated with the interests of the team at heart. We asked the suppliers involved with this customer about their perspectives on being included: They considered the invitation an honor and a challenge to prove that they were appropriate participants. One individual in one supplier organization explained, "Clearly, a supplier that participates in an important customer forum from a self-serving perspective is not going to be invited back. And we want to be invited back."

The final two practices included in figure 16.1—the future and the external business environment—define the critical focus for successful supplier-customer relationships. Most business leaders would agree that if a firm consistently focuses on the future and on the needs and challenges of its markets and customers, it is probably an organization with bright prospects. The same is true for supplier-customer relationships; the best ones emphasize the importance of these two focal points around which discussions and interactions should take place.

A customer that achieves this focus is in a pivotal position. Far more often than not, it is the customer in the relationship that takes the lead role in setting the partnership's direction. And it is the customer that should have the strongest access to and awareness of the markets and organizations further along the customer chain. The customer can use these advantages to help its suppliers, or it can use its position to suppress the supplier's viewpoint. Best-practice customers work hard to ensure that their key suppliers share their portrait of future success and their understanding of customers' critical success factors. Often these organizations are rewarded by suppliers who bring insights of their own into the discussion.

The research that identified these best customer practices in fact reveals considerably greater depth; the assessment tool developed for use in evaluating the quality of a customer's environment involves many more themes and topics that have been covered here. Furthermore, the context of these practices changes from environment to environment—for example, between what is relevant to motivate contributions from an ingredients supplier versus a capital goods supplier. The twelve short entries in figure 16.1 and the subsequent examples of various customer practices provide just a quick snapshot of what goes into creating a strong environment where supplier-customer relationships flourish.

In figure 16.2, we measure against a benchmark those twelve supplier-customer practices most closely associated with relationship success, from the top going clockwise. These practices range from promoting joint information flow to collaboratively addressing margin management issues to establishing clear performance metrics for the supplier. The scores range across unsupportive environments (in the center), supportive environments (in the middle), and best-practice environments (at the outside of the diagram).

On the whole, the particular relationship mapped on the chart operates in a supportive environment. Corrective steps should be taken, however, to address the three areas that are unsupportive. The supplier and the customer together should determine how to encourage the supplier to become more fully involved—to take a "seat at the table" during important decisions. Additionally, there should be a stronger, coordinated focus on all the participants along the customer chain, and

Figure 16.2: Relationship Map

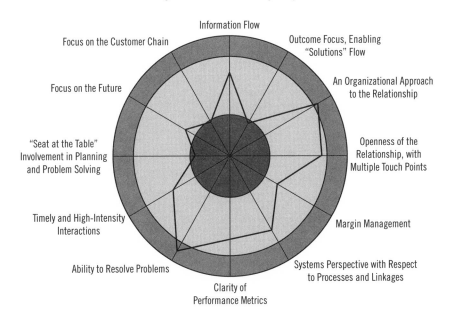

the supplier and customer must learn to invest time and attention in finding solutions, not simply addressing yesterday's problems.

Most customers exhibit a variety of behaviors toward their supplier relationships that range from unproductive to best practice. This varied pattern is not particularly unusual, as these two parties' interaction often evolved under various leadership regimes, without necessarily reflecting any deliberate or consistent strategy or goals. To develop an effective Go-to-Market Strategy, however, customer organizations must first identify suppliers that can contribute meaningfully to their value creation and value capture strategy, ones with whom they wish to build a strong relationship and then make a conscious decision to follow the best supporting behaviors.

SECTION III: IMPLEMENT YOUR GET-TO-MARKET PLAN

Chapter 17

IMPLEMENT YOUR VALUE CREATION AND CAPTURE STRATEGIES

Up to this point, we've developed a framework for value creation and capture and described its application to key go-to-market decisions about products, services, prices, acquisitions, and new markets. In experience after experience, the organizations we've worked with have found these concepts and practices to be appropriate and solidly based on market realities. But many clients have remarked that this approach will require a massive change within their organization—particularly in business markets in which the operational (e.g., engineering, research and development, manufacturing) and not the commercial focus has thus far dominated decision making and organizational structure.

One of our strongest beliefs is that great strategy unaccompanied by a great implementation process delivers little value. The harshest criticism a strategy team can hear is: "It was a great piece of work, but it's gathering dust on the shelves. It had no real impact on the organization and no ability to deliver rewards to shareholders." In our experience, a focus on the best practices for implementation is critical.

So in this chapter, we expand the framework to address best-in-class implementation plans that reflect the insights provided through case studies and the experiences of the business leaders with whom we've talked. This framework builds on specific details and prescriptions for managing the implementation process—ones that are closely aligned and built from the value creation and capture concepts we've already introduced. As we've synthesized our experiences and listened to business leaders in various industries, we've identified the principal elements of a Get-to-Market Plan. This plan must be defined, in a consistent and integrated fashion, in order for a firm to successfully implement the practices that will create profitable growth.

Virtually every business leader we've worked with first emphasized the goals and reasons behind the chosen strategy. Chris Curtis, Executive Vice President of the Buildings Business, Schneider Electric, focused on the clarity of the strategic intent, explaining, "You can't implement a generic strategy. It is essential that the strategy be clear in terms of what you are going to do." Other business leaders provided the same emphasis. Mike DeLano, Executive Vice President of Mitsubishi Electric Automotive America, observed that it is "critical to explain why the company will be better off with the changes." Al Saltiel, President of NC2 Global, a joint venture between Caterpillar and Navistar, cited an example from his years with Ford Motor Company: "Seventeen years later, I still remember the five key goals. They were simple and focused. Everyone got it." Such messages have permeated each of our discussions, and many of our case studies reveal the importance of having a strategy that is clear in its intent and purpose.

THE PORTRAIT OF SUCCESS

In our own practice, we've had significant success in working with businesses to construct a Portrait of Success as part of the transition from strategy formulation to implementation. The goal of the Portrait of Success exercise is to articulate your expectation for the future, using concepts and metrics that are familiar to the organization involved. Knowing how an organization describes itself is an important place to begin this process, so efforts must be made to define the descriptors used within the firm's various forms of communication. These descriptors typically differ from one firm to the next, spanning multiple dimensions, from performance metrics to organizational and operational metrics to metrics associated with its external presence and activities. Figure 17.1 suggests the high-level metrics used by one chemical firm in its self-portrait.

Once the metrics are defined, the challenge is to develop a Portrait of Success that forecasts what the future will look like if the strategy is successfully implemented. This process is demanding. Not only must the strategy and the associated business case be translated into details along many dimensions, but the translation must have internal consistency across its elements.

Tom Southall, Group President at Illinois Tool Works, Inc., said one of the key tests of strategy was "whether a business unit leader or a functional leader could sit down with his or her team and explain the strategy in the context of their jobs and responsibilities." Mark Weber, President of Federal Signal Corporation's Environmental Solution Group, commented, "Everyone has to know what the outcome is

Figure 17.1: Company Portrait of Success

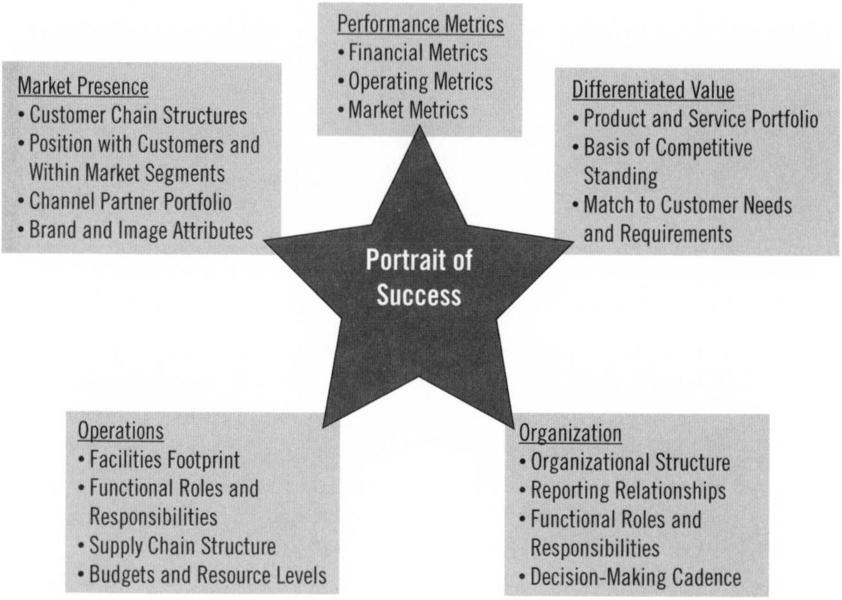

supposed to look like. If you know this, then you have a good chance of getting to it. If it's not clear, you can have a lot of people pulling in the wrong direction." Developing a Portrait of Success is a critical step in getting to the point where the strategy can pass such tests.

There are several other advantages to such processes. We've found that the process of painting the future often uncovers specific questions that have to be answered during the implementation process. The chemical firm whose descriptive metrics were summarized in figure 17.1 recognized during the process of constructing its Portrait of Success that there were significant options still open, particularly certain make-versus-buy decisions and options for the location of its manufacturing facilities. That such decisions had to be made was clear, but even after determining the strategic direction, multiple choices were open to our client. To evaluate such choices, the firm had to consider how each choice contributed to achieving its strategic goals. The process thus highlighted certain decisions that were open to the teams managing the implementation process, while other elements were clearly defined by the strategy itself.

THE GET-TO-MARKET PLAN

The elements of a Get-to-Market Plan fall within five major categories: Developing an Action Plan, Assigning Responsibility and Authority, Allocating Budgets and Resources, Communicating the Plan and Gaining Approval and Buy-ins, and Developing a Monitoring and Management Plan. There are numerous linkages among these five elements, and all must build upon and be consistent with the value creation and capture strategy. The following sections of this chapter provide insights as to how leading firms can develop these five elements of a Get-to-Market Plan.

WHAT AND WHEN: DEVELOPING AN ACTION PLAN

A Get-to-Market Plan must define the *what* and the *when* with a degree of specificity. It must let people know what to do when they show up for work on the Monday morning when implementation begins. Tom Southall noted that many failures occur when someone tries to implement a poorly developed strategy, one that hasn't been carefully thought out. He explains, "If you can't answer the questions that are going to be asked by the people involved, you aren't ready to begin implementation." Mark Weber observed, "The timeline has to not only spell out key milestones, but also define the interdependencies from one activity to the next—because if those aren't understood, you can get a lot of disconnects and delays." Many of the business leaders with whom we spoke described this as the basic blocking and tackling of good project management; they advocated the use of tools to help develop a clear and comprehensive action plan with sufficient detail so that all parties know what to do and when to do it.

Take, for example, one case that involved an important supplier to the global oil and gas industry giants. In a crucial emerging market that was rapidly evolving into one of the world's most promising oil and gas markets, the supplier's strategy required an increase in resources, investments, and talent. To grow and contribute to the large oil and gas customers operating in this market, the strategy dictated that the supplier quickly dial up the intensity of visible initiatives; this would showcase the supplier's commitment to customers in this area of the world. Even though this supplier had eleven different operations already established in this region, it needed its customers to become more familiar with its offering, especially considering the particular challenges that the customers faced in developing oil and gas in this market.

Together with the supplier, we developed detailed plans that involved twenty-two initiatives, ranging from hiring new commercial talent to creating customer-specific technology-sharing forums to establishing a technical training center for the customers' staffs. The initiatives were planned for completion along a set time frame: thirty days, ninety days, one hundred twenty days, one year. Assignments and roles were established among individuals across three continents, and resources were committed. During the implementation rollout, the

leaders held quarterly conference calls so the many functional participants could report on their progress. Each call was accompanied with
a project management tool that stipulated the initiative, the leader of
the initiative, the time frame, the status (e.g., done, underway, pending),
and related comments.

This example illustrates how important timing is—not only in
terms of the stages of the implementation plan, but also in the context
of the overall cadence of the business. The business leaders we've met
tend to agree. Randy Baker, President and CEO of Case IH Agricultural Equipment, Inc., noted that firms should be aggressive about
when they start the implementation process, so the plan can be implemented with momentum and consistency. He recommended matching the company's cadence in terms of planning processes and resource
allocation decisions, saying, "If annual plans and budgets are finalized in
January and you're still thinking about your recommendations in April,
nothing is going to get done for a year." Other executives emphasized
the importance of linking strategy and implementation to the company's long-term and short-term cycles. Tom Southall noted that his
company had a five-year strategy horizon and an annual operating
plan. By paying attention to both horizons, he felt his company could
"have a strategy and also [take] feasible one-year steps in the direction
defined by the strategy."

From our experience, timing of the implementation plan must
allow for quick, visible, impactful wins within the first six to twelve
months. Most plans, however—especially those involving product
development—must be developed over a longer horizon. In general,
strategies that are well implemented are completed within a three-to-
five-year time frame.

WHO: ASSIGNING RESPONSIBILITY AND AUTHORITY

A recent *Dilbert* cartoon[25] showed a project manager during a period of enthusiasm. In successive panels, Dilbert explains to a coworker, "She's tasting the sweet nectar of the illusion of progress. It's that euphoric feeling you get between the time you make a plan and the time some moron thwarts it." In our own experiences, there can be many reasons why someone thwarts a Get-to-Market Plan. Some of them have to do with a failure to understand the action items included in the plan; firms must be clear about the "Monday morning actions" that are required for successful implementation. Sometimes the problem is the misalignment of either individuals or organizational units; below, we discuss the challenges of communication and buy-in. Sometimes the decisions about the implementation team itself cause the problem. Numerous business leaders point to the decisions about *who*, asserting that they are just as critical as those about *what* and *when*.

In our discussions, we heard strong messages about choosing the leadership team that will drive the implementation process. According to Mike DeLano, his primary success factor was placing an "A Team" player in charge of the implementation process. That individual had to be passionate about the project and believe that it would yield a real contribution. He further emphasized that this leader had to have the full support of the executive team behind him or her. Mark Weber offered a similar thought: "Leadership can't be a committee. Someone has to have the assignment. The person has to be a strong project

---

25. *Dilbert*, Scott Adams, Inc., www.dilbert.com (also appeared in newspapers, January 27, 2008).

manager, able to keep clarity as to progress and tasks. The organization has to know who to turn to—and has to be confident when they do."

Mike cited many reasons that organizations fail to select an A Team leader, even when the project is critical to success: "A Team people are always busy, and you have to work to break them free from other assignments to take on [this new] project." Others pointed to the tendency to assign responsibilities for implementation by business function rather than on the basis of leadership and project management skills.

Also crucial to success: The executive team must play a starring role in backing the implementation team. Chris Curtis recommends that senior leadership be involved through a top-driven strategy agenda: "This agenda has to define what is a high priority, what is going to be taken on during a period, and what isn't on the [table]." Recognizing that projects can't be done in isolation, Chris believes that an agenda with a clear strategy empowers the team working on the project; it also brings resource discipline into the process and gets implementation on everyone's minds from the start. He noted, "Issues that might otherwise surface during implementation are going to surface earlier if you have all the various functions involved in a top-driven strategy agenda and review process."

Steve Henderson, President of Dow Automotive Systems, also argues that the organizational construct is key to success, saying, "Accountability has to be near the top for important implementation projects, and there has to be someone with 51 percent of the votes." To Mike DeLano, a major role of the executive sponsor is that of protecting the project leadership and team: "The executive has to go to the meetings, be the one who asks 'Why the delay?' and be ready to contribute to problem solving." Mark Weber observed that every organization looks at "what the senior managers *do,* not at what they say"—so if they aren't engaged, no one will see the project as important. These business leaders all link senior sponsorship to the monitoring process that we'll discuss later in this chapter.

HOW: ALLOCATING BUDGETS AND RESOURCES

One of the challenges to implementing a growth strategy was almost universally cited: ensuring that there are adequate resources and budgets for the project. While our case studies of successful and less-than-successful Get-to-Market Plans had numerous critical factors, resource and budget shortfalls were among the most frequently identified. A variety of suggestions surfaced as to how a firm should avoid getting into such circumstances.

Steve Henderson's organization has developed a process for examining the feasibility of the strategy in terms of budgets and other resources. Certain questions—such as "Can we afford it?" and "Do we have the right resources to do it successfully?"—are analyzed under a spectrum of assumptions about the business environment and the project itself. If the answer is no, then the team first searches for a workaround that changes the answer to yes. But if the answer remains no, then it's back to the drawing board to reexamine the strategy and find a feasible plan.

Mike DeLano told us his organization is normally focused on "details, details, details." Yet he noted that most major implementation projects are in fact characterized by "guess, guess, guess," because in reality, there are important uncertainties that cannot be predicted well in advance. As a result, he suggested, "A real contingency fund is a major contributor to success. A project budget has to anticipate every last detail, or else the budget and resources would be cut and the project is doomed to failure." An explicit line item that says, for example, "Contingency Fund, $500,000" gives the implementation team a chance to recover from the unexpected. The fund may never be used, but those who approve the budgets must decide whether they'd rather allocate a contingency fund or see the project derail when one of the guesses turns out to be off the mark.

Both Randy Baker and Tom Southall underlined the importance of clarity in both the longer-term strategy plan and the short-term operational plan. By recognizing that many implementation projects extend beyond a single year, a firm can adjust its operational plans to match business realities, without compromising the achievement of the strategic plan. Tom explained how the planning process can effectively use these two plans: "There is an important discipline about linking the strategic plan and the operations plan. When you do this, you don't lose focus on the strategy, because the 'one-year step' is an important part of operations." He also recognized that because most individuals' goals and incentives are tied to the operational plan, this linkage becomes a "communication that everyone pays attention to."

Randy also noted the importance of considering "normal cycles" for the specific elements of the implementation plan. In his industry, the cycle for product development and launch can be two years or more; the cycle for changes in market coverage involving channel partners or sales teams can easily be a year. Meanwhile, the cycle for initiatives involving pricing, promotions, and even service delivery can be as short as a quarter. The overall implementation plan and the associated allocation of budget and resources have to be consistent with these normal cycles. A Get-to-Market Plan can affect operations for a number of years, depending on the mix of initiatives in the plan. Most major plans include an overall strategic process that the firm will have to address in more than one operational cycle.

Even though it might be possible to fast-track certain implementation tasks, it is often necessary to institutionalize the change as well. Randy recommends continuing the implementation process for four to six months to build "operational habit" into the business. The task of operationalizing the change and translating it into the company's processes and culture typically requires additional resources and budgets.

Mark Weber emphasized the importance of depending on past implementation experience when establishing budgets and resources. Particularly for projects that are taking the firm in new directions—for example, a new manufacturing plant in eastern Europe or an initiative to begin selling product in China—the resource and budget requirements may be quite different from the averages that prevailed in more familiar environments. It is vital to refer to solid benchmarks that are explicitly relevant to any new settings and conditions that the implementation plan may bring.

In many business-to-business markets, building in new directions may require actions to be taken by third-party organizations along the customer chains, adding another dimension of resource and budget planning. Most frequently, this is a factor when the firm goes to market through dealers, distributors, wholesalers, or other channel partners; many other examples involve the firm's supply chain and even the firm's end customers. In our case studies, numerous implementation projects had been delayed because of the time required to bring third-party organizations on board. These organizations must also put into place their own implementation plans, using their own budgets and resources. Chris Curtis noted, "Too often, no one addresses the third party's value proposition during the strategy process." He argues that you have to examine the strategy not only from the standpoint of the company and the end customers, but from all participants' perspectives. He suggests, "Process maps help to think through third-party involvement, from demand creation and the factory floor to the end customer. Then you can ask who does what under the new strategy, why would they do it, and how long it will take them."

In a similar vein, Mike DeLano believes that when implementation requires collaboration from third-party organizations, the best approach is "to bring them clearly defined changes that are sure to work." But even then, he reflected, if you are going to ask channel partners to spend more or redirect resources, you have to have a compelling benefits statement and be ready—and have the time and resources—to sell, sell, sell the project. Al Saltiel sees a parallel with implementing change in matrix organizations, noting that while strategy should drive behavior, it takes time and resources to realize that in this type of organization. Too often, it is unrealistic to promote the project to other parts of the organization with the schedule and resources provided to the implementation team. The same considerations apply when the implementation process requires supplier organizations to make changes. These external units probably face other complicating factors, such as different planning cycles or linkages to other activities not understood by the firm driving the change.

In Steve Henderson's case, the implementation team came to recognize that its company was working on initiatives that were being repeated in customer organizations. The team went to these organizations, explained what was going on, and explained how both organizations could benefit from working in alignment. In this instance, "It became easy to understand why this was a win–win situation, why there was something in it for both parties." The two sides reached an agreement, developed revised action plans and resource commitments, and worked together toward an outcome that was a phenomenal success all around. The process required insight into the full customer chain through which the firm went to market, and the team had to adjust plans, schedules, and resources to effect collaboration.

One final insight about resource and budget planning came from Mark Weber, who noted that high costs often result when there are false starts on a project. Sometimes the false start is due to a "too early" launch, before all the elements of strategy are defined. Sometimes it is due to mistakenly thinking the right process is "ready, start, gain approval." And sometimes the false start is due to some external or internal factor that causes the organization to change plans with respect to the available budget and resources. In any case, Mark believes, "Too many projects fail when there is a head of steam, and then a stoppage for whatever reason. When that happens, it's really hard to get people to reengage." Moreover, the resources expended prior to the stoppage often were wasted, at least in part, as tasks have to be redone when the project is restarted.

THE LAUNCH: COMMUNICATING THE PLAN AND GAINING APPROVAL AND BUY-INS

Virtually all the elements of a Get-to-Market Plan tie in to the challenges of communications and gaining buy-in to the strategy. The business leaders we've encountered emphasized that this process has to be "up, down, around, and out"—spanning company executives, the people working in the trenches, the parts of the organization not directly associated with the strategy, and those outside of the firm whose involvement will prove to be important in some way. Steve Henderson noted, "Building trust in today's environment, in which people don't always trust one another or their corporation, is essential in order to [help them] become engaged and 'get on the ship.'" Steve argues that the inclusion process has to begin during strategy development, allowing people to come together, express their opinions, and provide creative ideas—so at the end, there can be 100 percent alignment with a solid base of facts and understanding.

To Tom Southall, communications about the plan are the most important factor behind its successful implementation. He believes that plans get implemented "if people understand them and understand their role in accomplishing the strategy"—and as we noted earlier, he tests his business unit leaders and functional leaders for their ability to create that understanding. Tom noted that people will ask questions such as "Why are we doing this?" and that the answers have to be relevant and achievable. "The strategy has to chart a meaningful future, one that accomplishes something," he explained.

Our own experiences with using tools and processes, such as the Portrait of Success concept described earlier, are consistent with his thoughts. When the portrait provides clarity about what is going to be different going forward, and about why that difference is a positive one, people can translate strategy into their own jobs and assignments. This process also helps to communicate what isn't part of the strategy and what isn't going to change. In numerous instances, the mistake of bundling too many unrelated assignments into a single plan resulted in its undoing. Beware, too, of individuals who use bundling as a way to further some idea of their own by linking it to the overall plan.

Business leaders understand that inclusion is essential to buy-in. Chris Curtis gave an example of a decision that resulted in changes to the priorities of his organization's sales team. While it wasn't possible to involve hundreds of salespeople or even dozens of sales managers in the strategy process, he made sure that the sales team was represented from start to finish by several individuals. This ensured that the sales team had input and that the rollout came from the sales leaders who had taken part in the strategy development. These sales leaders could immediately answer questions from salespeople—an important part of gaining their buy-in to the plan. Other business leaders told similar stories. Mike DeLano, for example, spoke of the success of a new software implementation, and how important it had been for business leaders to be seen using the system and explaining it to their organizations. Their inclusion among the early adopters was a powerful communication to the rest of the organization.

The process of inclusion must also extend to external organizations at times. This is probably most true in business-to-business markets where it takes contributions from multiple organizations along the customer chain to deliver value to end customers. Helping channel partners understand the Get-to-Market Plan and its implications for how they do business is critical to success. One business leader described a misfire that occurred because simple changes in such areas as order entry and order tracking had not been effectively communicated to channel partners.

Many businesses today source a significant portion of their overall product value from third-party suppliers. As one executive put it, "If half of your value comes from suppliers, probably half of your implementation is going to be in these supplier organizations—and probably more than half of your headaches will be there unless you have exceptional supplier-customer relationships." A range of other examples—from ingredient suppliers' product development initiatives that required changes in design, engineering, and application support to supplier initiatives for transferring production from one manufacturing site to another without disruption—underscore how critical it is to include third-party suppliers.

Understanding the environment in which buy-in has to take place is also important. On one occasion, we were asked by an organization to revisit a strategy that it felt had been a failure. The firm had invested in a process control innovation, expecting it to yield breakthrough gains for customers in such industries as oil and gas, pharmaceuticals, and beverages. The firm planned to sell its products into these industries, hoping that this concept would elevate its market presence by providing a high-value, integrated solution to certain process-related problems. After substantial investment in this technology, it was rolled out with considerable optimism based on the firm's testing and evaluation efforts. While the offering was much higher-priced than the current systems it sought to replace, the benefits calculation seemed dramatically in favor of greater initial spending. One business leader commented, "We expected shareholders to give us a prize at the next annual meeting." The market's reaction failed to support the firm's strategy, however, and the firm came to us to understand what had gone wrong—and to determine whether it was possible to achieve eventual success with this initiative.

Our research into business-to-business markets provided an

immediate foundation for understanding this outcome.[26] Clearly, there are multiple prerequisites for a firm to successfully sell its solutions to other businesses. One of these, certainly, is that that the idea itself is sound; business buyers are typically sharp-penciled analysts who can cull bad ideas from good ideas. Other requirements, however, can be as important as or even more important than the innovation itself. We've found that business buyers generally are very reluctant to introduce a new supplier's products and services into critical applications. They prefer to develop a strong foundation to the relationship first, a solid basis for predicting that the supplier can be counted on. This is true for both ingredients suppliers and suppliers whose offerings are critical to the customer's manufacturing and business processes.

It was the lack of such a foundation that had thwarted our client's success with its product initiative. Its new customers didn't really know this supplier, nor did they have any real experiences upon which to base confidence. Not only did the firm lack close relationships with its prospective customers, but this innovation was distinct enough from its traditional offerings that even a supporter could have questioned the supplier's ability to deliver the product and support its customers. One prospective customer told us, "The idea was certainly intriguing, and we're going to watch to see whether [this supplier] is able to create a track record elsewhere. If we gain some confidence that they can make this work, we'll be a fast follower. But right now, there are just too many unknowns for us to take the risk." This customer firm, along with two other organizations that we interviewed, clearly communicated a willingness to work with our client to test

---

26. Atlee Valentine Pope and George F. Brown, Jr., *Best-in-Class Behaviors in Business-to-Business Relationships* (Evanston, IL: Blue Canyon Partners, Inc., 2007).

the concept in a controlled setting, with the possibility of subsequent adaptation should the idea prove to be successful. So the problem was not in the strategy per se, but rather in the firm's failure to first develop relationships and build confidence in its ability to deliver on its promises. This approach is neither simple nor quick, but in initiatives such as this one, it is key to success.

A revised implementation plan emerged from this process, and it was considerably different from the original one. The time frame was lengthened so our client could develop relationships, and it was able to create a few reference successes with the organizations that were willing to test the concept. Ultimately, after an extended period of time, the firm became successful based on its revised Get-to-Market Plan. In the business-to-business environment, firms commonly learn that gaining buy-in from the participants along the customer chain—both inside the organization and on the outside—may itself be a major challenge during the implementation process.

CONTINUOUS LEARNING: DEVELOPING A MONITORING AND MANAGEMENT PLAN

The four elements of the implementation plan described above provide the basis for a fifth element: a monitoring plan to support it. Among the first and most important metrics that must be monitored is progress toward the goals stipulated in the Portrait of Success. The question "Are we getting closer to our goal?" is one that occurs with high frequency. The four elements of implementation provide the remaining metrics: "Are we on schedule?" "Have the tasks targeted for this period been completed as expected?" "Are we on budget?" "Is everyone who is part of the implementation process completing their assignments?" Business leaders emphasize the importance of building a clear scorecard that allows everyone involved to quickly gain answers to all these questions.

What is done with this information was emphasized in our interviews as strongly as the information-gathering itself. We heard from business leaders that the purpose of monitoring is to allow for changes in order to realize the established goals of the Get-to-Market Plan. The monitoring process, therefore, has to involve a focus on *why* things were off track (and often, why they are on track) and *how* the plan's elements should be adjusted.

Chris Curtis observed, "Monitoring and management must be timely. Quarterly reviews are critical to keep projects on track, with the executive team fully involved in the process." Chris advocates the explicit use of scorecards: "I'm a big believer in scorecards. The process of building them is valuable in and of itself, and they help to keep everyone on track, both those doing the implementation and those managing it." Mark Weber agreed, saying, "High-frequency reviews with senior management not only demonstrate the importance of the project, but also provide a forum for problem solving and cutting through issues."

Steve Henderson spoke about the need to plan in advance for the monitoring process: "I always look for killer variables, those one or two factors that can undermine a plan. They can be large or small—competitive actions, prices of inputs, turnover in the organization—any number of things. But you have to know what can derail the project and then monitor those factors carefully."

We tried this idea with a client, providing the project team with three descriptions of a derailed project and asking each individual to write a paragraph about why that scenario had taken place. Twelve people provided answers, including both executive team members and those in leadership roles on the implementation team. For the first scenario, eight of the twelve answers offered the same explanation. For the second scenario, seven of the twelve were similar. And for the third scenario, ten of the twelve answers focused on the same cause. The team concluded that it had identified its killer variables, and it then focused on how both the plan and the monitoring process could address them. One participant later dubbed this the "Portrait of Failure" process.

"Planning for some successes through implementation" is an important part of building a solid monitoring process, according to Mike DeLano: "The best outcome is when a success motivates everyone to say, 'This is working. Let's continue.'" Mike believes that the implementation team has to be proactive in setting mileposts and in thinking about what interim successes it can achieve. No one is going to be fooled by an interim success if the project is far off course, he noted. But public, early successes build champions and motivate the team, while failures and even the lack of any successes can bring out the negatives and the opponents.

Al Saltiel noted that a solid implementation plan can attract other parts of the organization as it unfolds, as long as the plan is clear and interim reports show progress. Day-to-day business—pricing decisions, channel decisions, etc.—naturally will continue in any company, and a good plan allows the organization to "connect the dots" so things fall into place consistently with the plan. By being involved in the monitoring process, the organization can help supply the information necessary to achieve this. We've seen business leaders at the end of a milestone presentation ask, "Is anything going on that is inconsistent with this? Is anything going to cause a conflict in the future?" One individual, after a presentation that showcased a project solidly on track, answered, "Houston, I think we've got a problem." Surfacing that disconnect well before the potential problem emerged turned into the most valuable part of that project's monitoring process. It never would have happened if the monitoring process had not drawn in leaders from across that company's organization.

One client, faced with a strategy to reach a new market segment, recognized that its implementation was going to trigger responses from the competitors already serving that market. In an attempt to get ahead of such responses and prepare the team to react quickly, the firm asked us to develop a competitive simulation. Based on our research about the industry and its participants, we developed briefing books and worked with the teams that would play the key competitors in the simulation. These team members knew the business well, and their years of experience started them off with a strong sense of how each competitor typically behaved under various circumstances. The simulation involved a series of rounds, with each team making decisions based on information about the market as well as the team's own performance.

From this process, the firm developed some clear insights about the likely shape of competitor responses to its entry strategy; it was able to identify signals that it felt were important to recognize about competitor decisions. The firm also constructed contingency plans that it used as the months progressed to quickly respond to competitor actions; thus its decisions remained consistent with its own goals and with the evolution of the business environment. The firm's leaders credited this simulation with enabling them to anticipate the challenges they would face during the initial period of market entry. It would be able to manage the process proactively, rather than always reacting after the fact to unanticipated changes. The process allowed the firm to view the actual implementation, in the words of one executive, "as our second time around doing this." We viewed this effort as a breakout approach to monitoring and managing implementation.

In collaboration with another organization, we reviewed six major implementation projects that had been undertaken over the past ten years. Each was considered to be complex, involving substantial budgets and time frames of a year or more—often substantially more. The initiatives varied in purpose, from the introduction of an enterprise software system to entry into a new geographic market. Together we reviewed numerous variables, comparing the assumptions in place when implementation started with the post-implementation reality. Figure 17.2 summarizes five of these factors along with our assessment of the initial forecast's accuracy.

Recognizing that any forecast involves a lot of "guess, guess, guess," the overall track record reflected across these five variables is quite good. The number of substantial differences cited between the original forecast and the reality was only one or, in the case of competitor products and technology, zero. But along almost every dimension, surprises occurred. Some of these (e.g., the post–September 11 economic environment) were driven by extraordinary external factors. Others (e.g., the entry of a foreign competitor or the shift of a major competitor from a wholesale model to a direct sales model) at best could have been guessed at, although in neither case was the evidence available to anticipate those decisions. And still others (e.g., a major change in one end market's structure) appeared even in retrospect to be, in the

Figure 17.2: Accuracy of Initial Forecast

	Number of Events Where Original Forecast Remains Substantially Correct	Number of Minor but Important Differences between the Forecast and Reality	Number of Substantial Differences between the Forecast and Reality
The Economic Environment	4	1	1
Identities of the Key Competitors	5	0	1
Competitor Product and Technology Offerings	4	2	0
"20-80" Mix of Largest Customers	4	1	1
Customer Chain Structure	5	0	1

words of one executive, "still hard to understand, and impossible to have predicted."

Our own reflections on this process were focused far more on monitoring than on forecasting. It is important to do as good a job as possible in outlining the assumptions that will drive elements of the implementation process. Yet it is equally important to recognize that some things will change while implementation is taking place. Knowing what changes to anticipate—and thinking through your responses to the inevitable surprises—can be a significant advantage. Our review of major success stories and creative insights from business leaders suggests that it is possible to go far beyond just monitoring implementation and making changes as appropriate. By taking proactive steps, a firm can ensure that its monitoring and management process creates a learning advantage for the implementation team.

There is more to implementation than just tracking progress and revising plans. "Individual objectives are an important part of any monitoring plan," according to Tom Southall. When assignments are tied into people's objectives and individual measurements and reward systems, he argues, "It has to matter to them. When they believe it is a key part of their job, something that they are supposed to spend time and attention on, they are going to monitor progress and surface roadblocks."

The business leaders we spoke with emphasized that the company's culture and the project's complexity had to be considered during development of the monitoring and management plan. Chris Curtis noted that thinking about whether there was a match between the strategy and the company's culture can guide the implementation plans and determine the level of attention required throughout the monitoring project. Randy Baker noted that in the most challenging situations, where major changes were required, implementation has to occur rapidly and an enormous level of attention must be given to the process. Mark Weber focused on the need to intensify monitoring when the project gets into territory that is unfamiliar to the organization and the implementation team—if necessary, bringing in "the right kind of gray hair" and probing deeply into situations that aren't comfortable. Each of these recommendations bears directly on how the monitoring and management process is handled.

Best-in-class strategy development must be accompanied by well-thought-out implementation plans. If it is not, the best ideas to create and capture growth will stall, sputter, and fail. A deliberate, paced implementation plan—led by the right team under strong management direction and with adequate resources—is the only approach that will successfully transform strategy into action.

Chapter 18

SUCCESS STORIES: INSIGHTS FROM IMPLEMENTATION CASE STUDIES

In the previous chapter, we introduced the general framework for a firm to follow in creating a Get-to-Market Plan that implements its value creation and capture strategy. Since each organization faces a unique set of challenges, however, business leaders must adapt this framework for a specific situation. The best way to accomplish this is to learn how other companies have used the framework to define their own Get-to-Market Plans. Following are three extended case studies that provide insights into the implementation process from a variety of industry perspectives.

CASE STUDY: A BUILDING PRODUCTS MANUFACTURER

This first case study involves a firm that manufactures a key product sold into new construction projects for various types of facilities. This firm, which holds a leading position within one major segment of this market, decided to investigate whether it made sense to enter another significant segment in which it had only rarely made sales.

New market initiatives such as this one offer a particular challenge for implementation plans: The obvious characteristic of a new market means that the firm must become involved in activities that, to some degree, it is not presently doing. That was certainly true in this case. The firm took pains to understand the market segment and develop a successful Go-to-Market Strategy, and these efforts immediately defined numerous challenges along essentially every element of strategy—products, services, brand, pricing, channels, and business systems. But despite the challenges posed by this new market, the strategy process uncovered clear opportunities for this firm to create value and concurrently capture value.

One element of this firm's Get-to-Market Plan was particularly complex, offering insights into best-practice approaches to implementation. This element of the implementation plan involved the channels through which this firm would reach its new market segment.

This firm traditionally had gone to market through third-party distributors, in part because its end customers typically bought its products as part of a bill of materials that involved products from numerous other manufacturers. The distributors' contributions to value creation involved the ready availability of these varied products, among other services. The firm's distributor authorizations were for specific geographic territories, and the distributors had exclusive authorizations within those regions. In many ways, this firm manifested the ideas described earlier about how best to bring channel partners into the value creation process.

The Get-to-Market Plan developed for the newly targeted market segment also involved distribution channels, but the firm's analysis suggested that the current distributor base had only a limited presence and a modest track record in the new market segment. As the implementation project began, the firm faced some challenging issues involving third-party organizations.

The channel team assigned to this implementation project first developed a profile of the channel environment across the various regions that the firm planned to serve. For each region, the team characterized the situation by first evaluating the performance of the firm's distributors in its traditional market segment. It then created a scorecard that assessed each distributor's readiness for the newly targeted segment, examining six dimensions (e.g., complementary product lines carried, response time, end customer relationships) that had been identified as important to success. Using an analytic structure similar to the (simplified) table seen in figure 18.1, each of the existing distributors was classed into one of four categories.

Figure 18.1: Classification of Distributors

	Has Key Competencies Necessary for Success in Newly Targeted Segment	Does Not Have Key Competencies Necessary for Success in Newly Targeted Segment
Is Performing Strongly in Traditional Market Segment	Extend Authorization to Cover New Segment	Discuss Possible Co-investment Initiative Targeting New Segment
Is Not Performing Strongly in Traditional Market Segment	Link Authorization in New Segment to Proactive Efforts to Achieve Improvements in Traditional Segment	Do Not Extend Authorization; Review Current Relationship to Define Path Forward

The assessment focused on the ability of the distributor to contribute to the value creation and capture process, both in the traditional market and in the newly targeted market. Figure 18.1 also suggests the basis of the implementation plan, which was carried out by the team in a very deliberate and structured fashion.

First, team members met with those distributors that exhibited strong current performance and the right competencies for success in the new market segment. This category included distributors that covered slightly more than 50 percent of the targeted market. The firm previewed its strategy with these distributors, taking care to keep details confidential until the overall initiative was announced. The distributors were told of the opportunity available to them, and expanded agreements were put into place with these organizations. During the planning period, the implementation team had determined that no conflict of interest existed among these firms in terms of their other supplier relationships, so this potential issue did not surface in the case of this action plan. For this community of distributors—which seemed to operate along the guidelines suggested by Steve Henderson when he said, "If the need is well defined, you can usually bring people on board with a combination of facts, good communications, and clarity as to why it works for both organizations"—the message was one of opportunity and collaboration.

This first phase of implementation yielded some major benefits. Discussions with these distributors yielded a few very good ideas that were incorporated into the overall implementation plan. One of these significantly simplified another task laid out in the implementation plan. A second major benefit came to light when several of the distributors were able to identify and provide introductions to distributors in other regions that fell into the other three categories of the assessment table seen in figure 18.1.

The most significant benefit realized from these discussions with channel partners was a friendly, familiar environment within which to test the many other elements of the implementation plan. Far too often, when implementation involves third parties, newly acquainted organizations are reluctant to engage in fully open communications. That was not the case for these long-standing partners. When this firm heard of a few gaps in its value creation plans, it was able to quickly address them without any adverse impacts on the schedule or the results. The majority of these issues surfaced rather quickly during the discussions with these distributors, who were able to spot the problems from their own vantage points far more easily than had been possible for the manufacturer. Using existing relationships as a test bed for implementation plans can turn into a major advantage for a firm.

Distributors within the two off-diagonal categories reflected in figure 18.1 each required distinct treatment. The distributors that were strong performers in existing markets, but that lacked the key competencies for the newly targeted market, were approached with a concrete, distributor-specific action plan for discussion and review. This category included distributors for just over 30 percent of the targeted market. This action plan defined the path by which these distributors could come up the learning curve to the point where they could anticipate success in the newly targeted market. Included in these plans were, for example, the distributor's commitment to send its technical staff to the supplier's training sites and its willingness to invest in continuous training as new products were launched. The manufacturer defined its own investments in this initiative—online tools such as easy-to-use training scorecards—and those that it expected its distributor partner to make. The pathway was portrayed positively but honestly, and considerable detail was used in describing the distributor's business model and financial outlook in this new market. These distributors were given the opportunity to gain the new authorization, but only in the context of an agreed-upon investment plan and timetable.

Most of the distributors in this category became excited about the opportunity offered by this newly targeted market and, after some discussions and back-and-forth, agreed to the action plan. The implementation team worked closely with each distributor team during the implementation process, to ensure that the necessary actions were successfully implemented in each partner organization. Later, individuals on both sides of these relationships reported that the process had been exceptionally healthy for the overall relationship, not just the elements associated with the new market.

A few distributors in this category, however, determined that they did not want to participate in the initiative to reach the newly targeted markets. Their reasons varied but had far more to do with the distributor organization than with the existing relationship or the actual business concept at hand. The manufacturer turned to new relationships in those few regions, but was able to do so with sensitivity; the process ensured that there would be no conflict with its existing distributors.

The third category involved distributors that showed performance shortfalls but had strong potential for the newly targeted segment, accounting for just under 10 percent of the targeted market. Discussions were held with these distributors after the vast majority of authorizations in the first two categories were either in place or nearly so. The opportunity was discussed as a win-win outcome, but the manufacturer mandated a first step to address the problems that were thwarting success in the market currently being served. Some frank exchanges ensued, and once again some ideas were introduced that would be relevant to success in the newly targeted segment. More important, the "carrot" represented by the new market proved to be a motivator in correcting existing issues. Mike DeLano's advice was highly relevant here: Show third parties simple changes, avoid complicating their lives, don't ask them to spend more or to redirect resources without offering a clear benefits statement, and be ready to "sell, sell, sell" the project. The distributors in this category had to be motivated to engage and to address significant issues relating to their businesses. Before authorizations were eventually granted to distributors in this category, performance benchmarks had to be met in both markets. In order to sustain the relationship, these distributors had to adhere to the incentive programs with trigger points related to sales in the existing market.

The final category—involving distributors that were neither performing currently nor positioned well for the newly targeted market—offered a fascinating opportunity for this manufacturer. Members of the firm's leadership team noted that these distributors had "probably lived in that position for a long time," regularly filling the lower performance quartile. This initiative provided an opportunity to kill two birds with one stone. The implementation team screened alternative candidates for authorizations in both market segments, and the manufacturer replaced existing poor relationships with new ones that offered strong prospects for success in both segments. The dual authorizations were a major motivation for new distributors that wanted to join this firm's channel network, and the implementation team garnered participation from the company's leadership in order to ensure that these new relationships began on a positive note.

The outcome of all these efforts has been a major success story for this firm. It has developed a strong position in the newly targeted market segment, to date exceeding the business plan upon which the strategy was approved. In the process, the firm strengthened its relationships with its key channel partners and even resolved some issues that were limiting performance in its traditional market.

CASE STUDY: A MACHINE BUILDER

Our second case study follows a firm that manufactures capital equipment used on factory floors around the world. This firm, the leader in its own industry, is viewed as the preferred supplier by customers in industry after industry, from the developed markets of Western Europe, North America, and Japan to emerging manufacturing centers in China, India, Mexico, Eastern Europe, and elsewhere. But the firm faced a challenge: Some elements of its technology base were maturing, and competitors emerging in several markets were able to produce products with virtually identical physical attributes and performance. In order to sustain its commitments to research and development and to continue to reward its shareholders, this firm undertook a strategy project with one overriding goal: to identify how to address the challenges of a partially aging technology base.

Once again, our research yielded some important insights. Some of these were quite reassuring. For example, there were market shifts toward technologies in areas where the firm's leadership position was unchallenged. Others were less reassuring. Some customer segments were quite capable of operating with "1950s technology" and were almost certain to use price to decide among suppliers offering that equipment. Once again, the strategic recommendations were complex; decisions would have to be made about specific segments of the market and across the elements of Go-to-Market Strategy, as appropriate for each segment.

And once again, a certain strand of the firm's Get-to-Market Plan was particularly complex, offering insights into best-practice approaches to implementation. This element of the implementation plan involved the way this firm surrounded its products with high-value services.

The information developed during the strategy project identified the purchase decision drivers of customers in certain key market segments when they were faced with the product lines incorporating this aging technology. As is suggested by figure 18.2 (again, a simplified

Figure 18.2: Purchase Decision Drivers

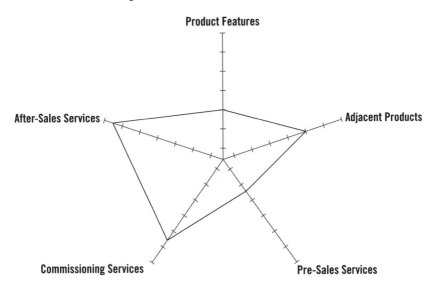

version), significant weight was given to two categories: Commissioning Services and After-sales Services. More weight was given to the availability of compatible Adjacent Products than to Product Features.

From a strategy perspective, this insight came as a surprise to the firm, which had gotten into a cycle of cutting back on services so it could respond to competitors' price points for similar product offerings. It was, however, a positive surprise—it defined a pathway toward sustained success with these products in these market segments. The firm could now respond to these customer messages about what contributions they valued. The real challenge was yet to come, however, when the firm addressed this element of its strategy during the implementation process.

Two aspects of this firm's implementation process provided challenges it had to meet. First, the firm needed to differentiate its position by offering best-in-class services to customers in these market segments, particularly during the commissioning process and in the after-sales environment. Research done during the strategy process provided some guidance, including clear messages about why these particular services were important to customer organizations and details on exactly what the customer needs were. The question that the implementation team had to address was how to provide these services.

To answer this question, the team decided to develop benchmark insights from firms that had faced similar challenges in different business environments. It realized that while its products were probably the best available in its own industry, its offerings were not sufficiently differentiated from its competitors'. Internal discussions also revealed that the service regime in place within the firm was at least a decade old. Mark Weber's comments—about the leading firms in any industry needing to look elsewhere for experience and advice—are relevant here: Someone else, somewhere, has gone through similar experiences, and if you can learn from them, you're way ahead of the game.

This firm used a benchmarking process that involved three major phases. First, for each of the major service components identified as important during the strategy process, the firm undertook a traditional benchmarking effort. It identified firms across relevant industries that were viewed as exceptional in providing such services; then it conducted research and discussions to learn the lessons that had yielded success in these other environments. Second, the firm focused on another offering that customers in these market segments viewed as important: the availability of compatible adjacent products. As part of this benchmarking effort, the firm investigated how other firms had linked services to a connected package of products. In this context, it identified valuable lessons about how to combine products and services into a solution that created value for its customers. We'll return to the third phase of this investigation shortly.

Backing up, the other implementation challenge facing this firm was to ensure that customers would reward the firm for its service contributions. As one company leader noted, "It's not a success if we add a lot of costly services to the mix and have to meet competitor prices in order to win the business. We can win the business based on our brand if we're willing to meet market prices. Services have to be viewed as creating value by our customers, value that they will pay for. Otherwise, all we're doing is eroding margins even further and faster than is otherwise taking place."

The strategy process revealed the weighting given to price relative to the other factors summarized in figure 18.2. The message from customers was fairly consistent: "When we know we're getting value via services and the overall offer, we can get beyond price. But oftentimes we don't see any difference from one competitor to the next. We can't justify a higher price on the basis of a prayer. There has to be something concrete to justify not going with the lowest bid."

The implementation team, looking at this metric from the perspective of its customers, worked to detail the total cost of ownership associated with the products and services involved. Through this process, it was able to quantify how total costs over the product's life cycle varied as a function of many factors, not just the initial acquisition cost. This life-cycle cost model addressed the time required to complete the start-up cycle, the costs of equipment upkeep and repair, the cost of repair parts, the degree to which efficiency varied as a result of preventive maintenance, the cost of downtime as a function of reliability and repair cycles, and numerous other factors. What it learned during this process was that the product's initial cost was only about 30 percent of its life-cycle cost. When the complete analysis was considered, many other factors were just as important as—or more important than—the first cost.

The insights from this analysis of the customer's total cost of ownership were connected to the third facet of the benchmarking effort. Recognizing the importance of total cost of ownership, the firm sought to learn lessons from other environments. How had other firms gotten customers to recognize and reward their contributions in the later phases of a product's life cycle? The discussions around these success stories involved not only what the firms had done to create a life-cycle cost advantage, but also how they had communicated this to their customers.

Two implementation lessons were especially valuable to this firm. First, this process underscored the value of information. In some industries, there was a legacy of sharp-penciled analysis, based on carefully compiled information about the life-cycle performance of various competitors' offerings. Examples were drawn from diverse industries such as electric utilities and freight logistics. The second lesson was about suppliers that had an advantage in terms of total cost of ownership: They could often embed that advantage in terms of their offer, translating the status of the cost advantage from "just another claim" to "a part of the contract." Examples of this type of strategy ranged from firms using differentiated warranty terms to prove their advantage to firms that bundled services into the initial sale at a fixed price (in contrast to competitors that only offered such services "by the drink").

The implementation team took advantage of these lessons as it structured the service offerings and connected them to the other elements of Go-to-Market Strategy. The firm strengthened the service offerings provided to its customers, in several cases at a lower cost than anticipated as a result of the strategies learned from other firms. It developed a strong information base, with evidence compiled from various sources, and was able to argue its advantages in terms of life-cycle costs; it also identified ways to prove its claims through a combination of information and contract terms. It created "solutions offers" that included well-defined combinations of products and services that were available as options to its traditional product offerings. By combining the many aspects of the overall implementation process, the firm emerged in a far better position with respect to the challenges it faced in its key markets.

CASE STUDY: A MEDICAL EQUIPMENT MANUFACTURER

The organization in this case study had concluded that its new product development process was not achieving its goals. Several recent releases had failed to excite customers. One company leader had characterized their offerings as an exercise in "yawnovation." She portrayed the problems as broadly based: "I'm not sure that we know what to do, and even if we did, I'm not sure we know how to do it." As a result, the firm had launched an investigation into what its new product development strategy should emphasize and how it should manage the process. The executive team that commissioned this effort stressed the need for a seamless transition from knowledge to decisions to action. As one executive commented, "I hope we can't tell where the boundaries are between strategy and implementation. That would suggest we're finally on the right track."

The team assigned to this project included both external experts and a variety of participants from the firm, spanning several functional groups. The project involved quite a few parallel tasks. In particular, the efforts that focused on developing customer-written plans for product development provided enormous insight; the firm was able to define the features that customers felt would be most valuable in future releases of its core products. The firm was able to move from a focus on "the ideas that were gleams in the eyes of our designers" to a focus on "what really mattered to our customers."

Another of the team's tasks related to the development and

management of implementation plans. This particular effort centered on the processes used by this firm to manage its product development efforts. The firm had used a somewhat traditional "stage gate" approach to product development: When an initiative was approved, the firm set up a series of milestones. As those points were reached, management did reviews to determine whether the project was progressing appropriately toward the defined goals. "Go versus No Go" decisions were made at each milestone, with subsequent-stage funding depending on passing the hurdle. Because of the complexity of this firm's products and technology, however, some of these product development processes spanned long periods, many of them four years or more.

In many regards, this process incorporated appropriate ideas about how to manage implementation efforts. It included active monitoring with senior management involvement. Considerable information was developed for review at the various stage gates; this allowed the firm to bring its expertise to bear in order to solve any problems that had emerged and revise the plans when necessary. Plus, this firm had shown a solid understanding of how to manage complex implementation processes. There were, however, two major opportunities to improve this product development process.

The first of these opportunities builds upon the fact noted by Mike DeLano: "Implementation involves guess, guess, guess." This is especially true when the process lasts for many years and involves complex research and investigation—both characteristics that are common to product development and innovation projects. In our own experience, "guess, guess, guess" is often replaced by "surprise, surprise, surprise." Sometimes the surprises are pleasant; sometimes they are less so. But they always exist during implementation.

Not only are surprises ever present, but they also can change everything. A strategy by necessity is based originally on the best guesses and insights available at the time. As guesses evolve into knowledge, the strategy has to evolve in parallel. The product, service, price, and other strategy elements that accompanied the original "guess" may no longer be the right ones considering the emerging knowledge. So there is a need not just for a seamless transition from strategy to implementation but, even more demanding, for an ongoing cycle that links strategy and implementation. The firm in question supplemented the stage gate process to involve a review of the underlying strategy. In this way, it ensured that the key motivations for the product development charter remained accurate in light of the progress that had (or had not) occurred since the original plans.

The team working on this project documented three case studies of the firm's own product development efforts, each of which involved a disappointment for the firm. The team asked, "Would applying the evolved stage gate process have altered that outcome?" It determined that one of the three projects would have been stopped, while another would have been either stopped or redefined and redirected. Moreover, the executives who looked at the information said the decision would have been a no-brainer if this process been in place. One of them commented, "I will retire still wondering how we could have missed this."

This firm had a long discussion ahead of it: How could it make sure that the new process was going to be successful in blending strategy and implementation, especially for product development and innovation projects with long lead times? Company leaders came up with three guidelines that we view as important and valuable insights:

1. Following the strategy project and before implementation has begun, use risk analysis and sensitivity testing to define the factors most likely to drive the project off course. When the monitoring process is defined, specify the stage gates at which there is an explicit review of these "killer variables."

2. The individuals who developed the strategy must be part of the review process at key stages of implementation. They are the only people who can possibly know what is a show-stopper, what is important, and what just doesn't matter.

3. Incorporate into the stage gate process a review and assessment of new insights that have emerged. Study their impact on the initial elements of strategy and on the external elements of the business plan.

The first of these guidelines builds upon Steve Henderson's advice to figure out the killer variables—those that can undermine a plan. The second invokes Mark Weber's suggestion that the monitoring team include individuals with "the right kind of gray hair" to define what certain changes mean in terms of responses and eventual success. The third guideline introduces a new concept: At each stage gate, look not only at what has happened vis-à-vis the plan, but also at what has happened that wasn't ever considered within the plan.

The second major opportunity to improve the product development process addressed the question of external organizations. The firm involved in this case study had worked aggressively to keep its product development plans under wraps; its intention was to surprise the market and leapfrog its competition. As a result, the monitoring and review processes not only were 100 percent internal, but actually were managed on a need-to-know basis even within the firm. Was the process too inward looking?

When the project team developed the three case studies, as we noted above, two of the three would have been managed differently had the new process been in place. The third case study provided a different insight: This firm's customer chains were important. The project defined four stages between this firm and the final customers served by its products. These four stages (which varied from one pathway into the market to the next) included a mix of intermediaries and organizational units. The problem with the project was that the very concept in which the firm had invested was unacceptable to the decision makers three stages further along this customer chain. It violated these customers' existing concepts of how they would do business, by requiring them to work with multiple vendors instead of fostering the single-vendor relationship that they had defined as important. While that decision could be debated, it was the established practice of customers at that stage of the customer chain—they wanted a single platform, a single source, and a single set of protocols across the procedures involved. The product concept that our client had developed would have required that these customers remove an offering from the "single platform, single source, single protocol" system. The product failed because the client's customers were unwilling to deviate from this system.

What the team learned was that the customer chain cannot be ignored in business-to-business markets. The success of a strategy will depend on the reactions of the organizations involved at every stage of the customer chain, and their inputs must be considered at every stage of the implementation process. In the third case study described above, the initial plan involved an offering that was consistent with the critical "single" concept. As implementation progressed, there were surprises, many of which were positive, but one of which decoupled the product from that "single" environment.

That this change was critical to customer acceptance was not recognized. It can be argued that this fact should have been uncovered during the strategy process and included among the killer variables, but that had not been the case. Our own experience is that the challenge of uncovering "God-given" assumptions is among the most difficult elements of any strategy development process. This was a case in point. In literally scores of discussions, the "single" mandate never surfaced. It was a given to the interviewees—and an unknown to the interviewers. Tom Southall's advice is important here: When you need information and insights from third parties, you have to include them in the process. This was a situation in which that type of involvement would have paid great dividends.

So this consideration never made it to the killer variable stage, even though it was in fact one. And even the augmented stage gate process, while it addressed important deficiencies of the previous process, would have never uncovered this problem. Only involvement of third parties from along the customer chain would have produced the reaction that could have helped: "This is insane. It will never fly." In the end, our client concluded that it needed to engage the customer chain in product development implementation, not just in product development strategy. Every company leader to whom we've spoken suggests that this is a major challenge. Chris Curtis's comment—"Too often, no one addresses the third party's value proposition during the strategy process. They figured out what was good for the company and probably what was good for the end customer"—summarizes this reality quite well. Especially when things change, figuring out the implications for organizations and decision makers at every stage along the customer chain is critical to success.

The new product development strategy developed and implemented by this firm differed considerably from the processes it had in place previously. The firm initiated projects driven by external, rather than internal, motivations. It began to change the implementation processes that had guided decisions over the years, from concept to launch. It began to incorporate new factors at each decision gate; it encouraged involvement, rather than secrecy, of the organizations at subsequent stages of its customer chains. While results are preliminary at this point in time, the firm has enjoyed two major successes in the recent past—a marked departure from the earlier track record.

A BLUEPRINT FOR SUCCESS IN DEVELOPING GET-TO-MARKET PLANS THAT SUCCEED

We've provided numerous ideas and examples of how firms can develop and implement their Get-to-Market Plans successfully. These concepts can be summarized with a "top ten" list for firms as they manage the transition from the value creation and capture strategy process to implementation plans that are positioned for success.

1. **You can't overdo the basics—focus on the "blocking and tackling" and build a solid implementation plan.** One interviewee noted that all the world's maxims should be brought out and forced onto the implementation planners: "Don't neglect the

details," "Measure twice, cut once," "Plan the work and work the plan," "Check your work," etc. The structure and elements of an implementation plan (as in figure 18.2) are the usual suspects; most of the horror stories we've heard involved at least some short-coming in addressing one or more of these elements. The starting point for a successful implementation process is a solid implementation plan that can be effectively and clearly communicated to the organization, with sufficient detail about what is being done and why it will benefit the organization.

2. **Treat implementation as an important process, and develop competencies around implementation.** Leading corporations across many industries underscore the complexity of implementing a strategic plan. The diversity of the "most critical factors" cited by company leaders further emphasizes the degree of difficulty that the leaders and members of an implementation team will face. Developing an understanding of best practices in implementation, in general and in the context of a particular corporation's culture and organization, can pay enormous dividends. This understanding should be taught to those who will lead or be significantly involved in major implementation processes, through a combination of formal education and on-the-job training. Managing implementation is too important to be left to learn-on-the-fly approaches.

3. **Arm the implementation team with appropriate tools and solid information.** Implementation projects involve all the elements of project management and organizational communication. Developing and/or taking advantage of the tools that facilitate such efforts can not only help the organization avoid simple mistakes and ensure coordination across a plan, but also facilitate the task of

keeping all participants and stakeholders on the same page. Various tools have been developed from one organization to the next, but all those we've shared are straightforward, enable various levels of details to be examined, and spotlight plan elements that required attention and problem solving, often through such simple systems as green-yellow-red scoring. Beyond that, in every company that we consider a best-practice firm when it comes to implementation, we heard a phrase like "This is the tool we've developed to manage implementation projects in our company"—emphasizing that these tools were well understood by the company's people and an accepted part of the organization's management processes.

4. **Connect the strategy team members and the lessons they have learned to the implementation plan and process.** The team that was involved in developing the strategy remains a vital source of insight during the implementation process. Several interviewees noted that probably only 10 or 20 percent of the content and knowledge that was developed during a strategy development process actually makes its way into the strategy or the initial implementation plan. Meanwhile, some elements of the remaining 80 to 90 percent might be the basis for avoiding problems during implementation. The firm can tap that expertise—through involvement on the implementation team or in the monitoring process, or at minimum, through reconnection—to address unexpected developments that occur as implementation proceeds. Some organizations schedule meetings with the members of the strategy team at key points during implementation; these individuals provide reactions to the implementation team's reports of progress and problems.

5. **Bring lessons from other environments into the implementation planning process.** Recognizing that virtually every implementation project involves venturing into unfamiliar territory, successful firms must identify and tap into other environments in order to glean information and insights. These sources not only provide direct factual content (e.g., "How long does it take to . . ."), but also best-practice insights (e.g., "In China, one key to success involves . . ."). A part of taking advantage of this idea involves cataloging the unknowns associated with the project and thinking about what sources might provide useful insights about these unknowns.

6. **Ensure that the team and its leadership are the right ones to achieve success, in terms of leadership skills, implementation skills, and key competencies.** All the messages about the "A Team," the "right kind of gray hair," etc., point to the fact that difficult implementation projects require exceptional leadership and teams. One business leader commented on companies spending significant sums on strategy development, but then turning over the implementation process to "their organization's current crop of homeless." While no one has suggested that great choices for the project team can overcome failure to address the other elements of the process, we're convinced that a strong team can do the right things right and address the inevitable surprises that occur during the implementation process.

7. **Manage the customer chains—internally and externally—that are in any way connected to the success of the implementation process.** Every project will eventually extend outside the business units that are directly involved in the implementation, both internally and externally. Firms can ensure that the project

doesn't fail at these important junctures by carefully cataloging those connections, developing insights about the implications for each of these organizations and business units, and developing a plan to motivate their involvement and collaboration in the project. Being able to answer the question "What's in it for me?" for all such organizations is a critical part of this process. Thinking through the process, timeline, and resource implications of this engagement can ensure that the overall project plan doesn't go off track because of the failure to forecast these dimensions of third-party involvement.

8. **Set up the implementation team for success, with realistic milestones, resources to address contingencies, and the ability to achieve some early successes.** This guideline argues for a succession of short steps to allow progress to be observed as it occurs. This method also enables the implementation team and the company's leadership to address and solve small, rather than large, problems. Plans that avoid unrealistic milestones and that provide adequate resources to address unexpected contingencies are part of best-in-class companies' preplanning for success.

9. **Preplan the monitoring process and minimize the degree to which the process ever becomes an adventure.** The numerous lessons we've heard about how to manage the monitoring process emphasize being proactive—spotting killer variables, role-playing competitor responses, developing a Plan B, etc. Such steps contribute not only by arming the company leaders who are monitoring and managing the process, but also by removing time delays from this process. Avoiding unnecessary delays due to unexpected events can be quite valuable to the eventual success of

implementation, particularly when the project has some degree of time sensitivity.

10. **Ensure that the organization's leaders are effectively involved and committed to success.** Leadership involvement is important for many reasons, from showcasing the project's importance within the organization to bringing the company's best talent to bear when problem solving is required. Such involvement cannot be either last-minute or occasional. It must begin early enough in the strategy development process to ensure context and content; it must involve a high-frequency set of interactions that contribute currency and timeliness.

Though the implementation process varies greatly from one firm to the next, certain ideas, such as those listed above, are essential to the success of the process in any business environment.

Chapter 19

CONCLUDING COMMENTS

We've covered a lot of ground in this book, from foundations to strategy to implementation. For those readers who've made the journey with us, we hope it has been productive and even enjoyable.

As it is neither possible nor necessary to summarize eighteen chapters any differently than we did in the introduction, we will not attempt do so. Rather, we'll conclude by citing three important lessons that we've seen over and over—lessons that can spell the difference between success and failure.

First, we cannot underscore too many times the importance of the foundations that we developed in section I. The concepts surrounding customer chains, the sources of value creation, assesment of value levers, and the behavioral approach to segmentation are behind all the ideas that have followed in later sections of this book. The most successful firms always return to these foundations and avoid other distractions. These firms know that their customers want them to be successful—and that if they put themselves into their customers' shoes, they'll be able to develop strategies for all parties to achieve a win. These firms also know that these foundations cannot be taken as a given; they change over time, they differ from one market to the next, and they evolve as a result of various external forces outside any firm's control. It isn't always necessary to return to square one, but it is always important to ask what has changed across these foundation elements and how that must be translated into other decisions.

Second, it is essential that firms develop an effective Go-to-Market Strategy. To do so, firms must consider everything from brand and product to pricing decisions to the third-party organizations that will have an eventual say in every firm's success. The most successful firms base these decisions on the foundations established in section I. They know that their decisions on products, services, pricing, sales models, and other factors must be driven by customer-written plans, ones that define how the firm can bring greater value to its customers than its competitors can. In addition, firms must develop a Relationship Advantage with appropriate suppliers, customers, channel partners, and other organizations up and down the customer chain. Far too often, we've seen these relationships become adversarial, dominated by zero-sum considerations rather than win-win considerations. Yet many other firms have amplified their own abilities to create and capture value by encouraging strong customer, channel partner, and supplier relationships. The firms that can build such co-destiny relationships can be confident of the rewards that investment will bring.

Our final focus is on implementation. When we started our firm, one of our major goals was to ensure that the work we did was translated into action, resulting in rewards to shareholders. We build from an action-oriented foundation, and we've tried to link that foundation very explicitly to the decisions faced each Monday morning when the company's employees show up for work. Those decisions span many job functions and responsibilities, whether they hinge on daily, monthly, or yearly decisions. But a focus on successful implementation of the strategy is as important as the focus on the right approach to value creation and capture. Along with the explicit linkages defined within our methodology, the insights from best-practice firms relating to implementation and strategic change can, we hope, help your company improve its skills along this critical dimension and reap the rewards of profitable growth.

INDEX

value levers for, 77–79, 82–83, 91–92, 96

Energy Star, 93

engine manufacturer, 33

Environmental Protection Agency, 93

equipment and consumables, 208–9

Europe, 188, 256

external business environment, 221, 229, 239–40

F

Fairfield Inn by Marriott, 125

The Fast and the Furious (film), 27

Federal Signal Corporation, 247

food industry. *See also* packaging supplier case study
    customer chains, 22, 23, 24–25
    family restaurant chains, 93–96
    foodservice distributors, 81–84, 131, 135–36, 138
    grocery business, 24–25, 77–79

Ford Motor Company, 246

Fuller, 129

furnace and air conditioning market, 8, 11–13, 19

G

GEICO, 197

Get-to-Market Plan, 9, 249. *See also* implementation

global markets, 84, 136, 139, 174, 187, 188–92, 218

Good-Better-Best product spectrum, 118–19, 122–26, 142

Good product offerings, 118, 119, 120, 125, 128

Go-to-Market Strategy, 9, 298. *See also* acquisitions; collaboration; competition;
    customer selection; price; product and brand strategy; services; suppliers

growth. *See also* acquisitions; customer selection
    challenges to, 17–18, 36, 41
    customer chain opportunities for, 23–25

H

Henderson, Steve, 253, 254, 257–58, 259, 264, 274, 287

high-technology industry. *See* technology industry

home builder market, 12, 19, 26, 65

homeowners in customer chain, 12–13, 19, 26, 65

ABOUT THE AUTHORS

Atlee Valentine Pope is president and cofounder of Blue Canyon Partners, a strategy consulting firm that helps companies grow. She has worked with clients around the world, coauthored more than 40 papers, and has been a guest speaker at numerous business events. Before building Blue Canyon Partners, Atlee served in leadership roles in several start-up ventures and was a vice president in global corporate finance with First Chicago. Atlee earned a BA from the University of the South in Sewanee, Tennessee, and an MBA from Northwestern University's Kellogg Graduate School of Management.

George F. Brown, Jr., is CEO and cofounder of Blue Canyon Partners, where his practice allows him to contribute to solving clients' business-to-business growth challenges. Prior to Blue Canyon, George held senior leadership roles in a number of organizations, including DRI/McGraw-Hill and ICF Kaiser International, and he served as the Theodore Roosevelt Professor of Economics at the U.S. Naval War College. He has published extensively in academic and business journals and testified frequently before Congress. George received his MS in Industrial Administration and his PhD in Economics from Carnegie Mellon University.